The Unappreciated Fisher Folk

James Glass Bertram

BIBLIOLIFE

International Fisheries Exhibition

LONDON, 1883

THE

UNAPPRECIATED FISHER FOLK

THEIR ROUND OF LIFE AND LABOUR

BY

JAMES G. BERTRAM

AUTHOR OF 'THE HARVEST OF THE SEA'

LONDON

WILLIAM CLOWES AND SONS, LIMITED

INTERNATIONAL FISHERIES EXHIBITION

AND 13 CHARING CROSS, S.W.

1883

CONTENTS.

THE UNAPPRECIATED FISHER FOLK.

THEIR ROUND OF LIFE AND LABOUR.

INTRODUCTORY NOTE.

IT was expected of Sir Walter Scott, when the author of
'Waverley' was in his prime, and his novels and poems were
undoubtedly *the* books of the period, that he would some
day devote his attention to the toilers of the sea, and weave
the round of fisher life, with its perils and privations,
its brief joys and prolonged griefs, into one of those
romantic narratives of which he had become the master
spirit.

It is certain the great novelist meditated at one time
a work of that kind, and that he employed himself on
several occasions in gathering such information as would
give reality to its details, as also in making those
studies of character in which he so much delighted. The
friends of Sir Walter Scott have now mostly all gone
over to the majority; and there can be only very few
alive to-day who have held converse with the "Lord
of Abbotsford." Probably Doctor William Chambers
was about the last of the men who knew Sir Walter,
and could have spoken from personal knowledge of
that great man's aspirations, but now the good doctor himself, after a life of much usefulness, is sleeping his last sleep.
It was the doctor's brother, however, Robert Chambers,

B

who told the writer that Sir Walter had intended at one time to write a story of fisher life and adventure, and that he had even gone so far as to mention his project to Constable, his publisher.

It is our loss that the author of the ' Waverley Novels ' did not include in that grand series of books, a narrative of the toils and troubles of those who try to find their daily bread in the treacherous waters of the ravening deep—other than *The Antiquary.* No pen can be thought of that would have touched the subject with greater felicity During the brief residence of Sir Walter at the fishing village of Auchmithie, on the Forfarshire coast, he had many opportunities of studying the daily round of fisher life. Twenty years ago there were persons in Auchmithie who remembered the illustrious visitor, and who took note of his anxiety to make himself acquainted with the eccentric people who formed the little community, in which for a short time he had taken up his abode, and some of whom were reproduced in the pages of *The Antiquary.* In the rude fishing village of Auchmithie in the time of Sir Walter, the fisher folk were unchanged from the days of a far back period, and even at this day they are still much as they were then—a peculiar people. The superstitions and curious manners and customs that had been handed down from generation to generation still prevailed—the observances connected with the births, deaths, and marriages of the people were insisted upon, and in all respects the fisher life of Auchmithie was typical, and represented in a broad sense the daily life of the hereditary fishermen and fisherwomen of Scotland. It is certainly in Scotland (and in Cornwall as well) that the life and labour of this hardy and industrious class of persons can be studied to the greatest advantage, and in some places even yet their daily round of existence rolls on much as it did a century ago. In Scotland, the patriarchal system of work is still largely maintained; in many Scottish fishing villages the family fishing boat is as much an institution as a family walnut-tree is in France. In a number of the English fishing ports the order of business is somewhat different from what we see in Scotland; there is less of sentiment and comparatively little of the superstitious element, but at Holy Island, Cullercoats and some other places the fisher class are much the same as we find them in Scotland or Cornwall. In Scotland, the fisher communities seldom receive any accession of new blood, and fathers and sons go on succeeding each other for many generations. The fisher folk intermarry in their communities, and so preserve those traditions of labour and the observance of those social customs which have become stereotyped among the people who go down to the sea in fishing ships.

It is interesting to know, moreover, that in nearly all fishing villages, whether they are in Scotland or in France, in Spain or in Holland, the life of the fisher people, as of course it can scarcely help being, is of the same complexion; a life mostly of hard work, much danger, and scanty remuneration. Yes, the fisher folk of France are the very brothers and sisters of those of Scotland, their manners and customs, their modes of life, and all that pertains to their dangerous occupation on the waters, being nearly identical. The various communities seem to have set themselves down in convenient places for following their avocation. There are villages and little towns upon the shores of the sea that nature seems to have destined for the abodes of fishermen; there is usually a natural harbour—" a bieldy cove," in which the little fleet of fishing boats finds, during all seasons, a happy refuge from fierce winds and battling waves.

It may not, perhaps, be generally known to those who

are not in possession of special sources of information, that in all fishing communities, the woman is head of the house, and nowhere, in all fisherland, at home or abroad, is this more the case than on the Firth of Forth   The Newhaven fishwife has become a celebrity, and she is indebted to King George the Fourth for much of her fame.   That monarch during his memorable visit to Edinburgh, in the year 1822, said to Sir Walter Scott, that some of the Newhaven women were the handsomest he had ever seen ; and her present Gracious Majesty has been likewise pleased to admire them.   Indeed, since the Queen's first visit to Edinburgh, the Newhaven fishwife, with her picturesque peculiarities and the dulcet notes with which she charms the public ear, as she cries her oysters (*Caller Ou*) has become quite a pictorial personage.   She has been painted in oil, modelled in card board, made up as a whisky bottle, given to children as a doll, printed in numerous *Cartes de visite*, and generally, has been made much more public all over the world than any other honest woman   She is a familiar figure in the Café Greco at Rome, as well as in the print shops of Berlin and Venice , and although the praises of the Newhaven fishwife with passing compliments to her "shapely shanks," and the sweet voice that made the heart of the Ettrick shepherd "dirl" with emotion, have been celebrated by Christopher North in the *Noctes Ambrosianæ*, it has not spoiled her, nor yet interfered with her determined and ceaseless industry. She is ruler over her household and chancellor of her husband's exchequer ; it is a saying, indeed, of the fishwives, that the woman who is not able and willing to work for a man ought not to have one.

The labour of the females in the olden time was heavy, but it is less so now that so much of the fish caught

by their husbands and sons is disposed of at the side of
the boat in wholesale fashion, to buyers from those
large seats of population, which are always demanding
supplies of fish, and are never able to obtain all they want.
Some of the fishwives make excellent auctioneers, they
possess a rude eloquence which is difficult to resist. The
fishwives of Newhaven and Fisherrow in the days of old
used to bear on their backs in baskets called "creels" large
burdens of fish daily to Edinburgh, with which they
wandered from door to door in search of customers—a
practice that still to some extent prevails, but which has
been largely rendered unnecessary by the increase of shops
for the sale of fish. Their achievements in fish carrying
have been often chronicled. When the boats were late in
arriving, two or three of the women would join in carrying a
heavy creel full of cod and haddocks, to Edinburgh. Each
woman carried the creel in turn, and by this means fish
have been heard calling in the streets of the modern Athens,
that had only been brought into Newhaven thirty-five
minutes before. Once upon a time, four women walked, or
rather "trotted," with a creel full of fish, from Dunbar to
Edinburgh, a distance of twenty-six miles, in five hours!
And after all, each hundredweight of cod and turbot
carried so gallantly could only realise a few shillings. A
big cod-fish for tenpence in those days was an every-day
bargain, whilst "fine caller herrin', three a penny," was a
stereotyped call of the fish hawkers.

In addition to Newhaven there are numerous other
quaint fishing communities in Scotland where the manners
and customs of the people are worthy of study. Newhaven,
from its proximity to Edinburgh, and the fame of its fish
dinners is often referred to, and is frequently visited by
strangers from the most distant places. All fisher folk, no

matter where they are located, whether at "Fittie" in Aberdeen, or at Portel, near Boulogne, or in the Rue de Pollet of Dieppe, are largely imbued with a feeling of superstition ; they can read the clouds at night or morning, and discern signs and omens in nearly every passing circumstance. They have their pet aversions, their likes and dislikes. In some villages the mere advent of a stranger would detain the men from going to sea for hours ; the impression of a mysterious foot on the sand has before now caused consternation in a fishing village ; the flight of a few harmless crows over their boats has struck terror to the souls of stalwart men who have faced death many a time and oft on the raging waters, and have courageously battled with the storm-king in the cause of the dear ones at home. In fisher villages it is the rule to wed within the community ; no fisherman would think of bringing home a "stranger woman," to be jeered at by his friends and companions. In some communities there is a wonderful scarcity of surnames, and identity is preserved by the use of what are called "to-names" (added to), or "nicknames" as they may be called ; thus a family of Fluckers, in which all the common Christian names have been over and over again exhausted, will be designated by some personal mark, as "gley'd Johnnie," or "dumpie (short) Johnnie," and so on *ad infinitum* through a long range of names of persons, places, and things ; such appellations being necessarily recognized in courts of law, and in all kinds of civil and criminal deeds and documents. The following is a rather curious example of the way of using a *tee* name. A fisherman of the name of Alexander Mair, who rejoiced in the nickname of "Shavie," being confined for a debt in the prison of Banff, had occasion to write to his wife at Portknockie, and some wag thus addressed the letter :

" Janet Euing, ' Shavie's ' wife,
Pray pay the cash and save his life,
For poor auld ' Shavie' is in jile,
An' distant frae you sixteen mile.
Portnockie Cullen."

Often enough these cognomens lead to little mistakes of
an irritating kind, but in all legal documents or communi-
cations of importance the nickname is always used as a
mode of identification.

It was a cause of surprise, when on a recent occasion
His Royal Highness the Prince of Wales entertained the
fisher people who were visiting the International Exhibition,
that the majority of those who had come from Scotland
were teetotallers, who would neither drink beer nor Burgundy.
It is not, perhaps, too much to say that at the herring
fishery a large number of the vessels are now what are
called " teetotal boats," on board of which no spirits are
ever taken ; and the men find they can fish quite as well
without supplies of whisky as when they took two or
three drams every night. It used to be a standing re-
proach to the Newhaven fishwives in the olden time that
they " drank," and there was no doubt a little truth in the
accusation ; after carrying about a load of fish weighing
from eighty to a hundred and twenty pounds they were
sometimes, as the saying goes, dead beat, and resorted on
occasion to "a dram " to restore their flagging energies.
When Sir Walter Scott witnessed the work performed by
the fisherwomen of Auchmithie—when he saw them rush
into the water to bring their husbands and sons ashore on
their shoulders—he was not surprised to learn that some
of them partook of stimulants. "You take a dram, I
perceive," said the author of ' Waverley.' " Oh, 'deed we dee
that, an' we hae muckle need o' 't tee ! " was the prompt and

unaffected reply. Many of the Scottish fisher folk are deeply religious; in some communities the men and women conduct a service of praise and thanksgiving, and the unlettered eloquence of a rude preacher of that class would sometimes shame the cultured rhetoric of the pulpit.

The conditions of their shore life, till within these few years back, was shameful ; the fishing villages of Scotland were as a rule devoid of all amenity, their sanitary surroundings were of the rudest and scantiest description ; dirt—otherwise "matter in the wrong place"—obtruded itself at every corner. Some improvement in these matters has now been happily effected, and the thin end of the wedge having been inserted, more perfect sanitary arrangements will doubtless follow in a short time. As we propose to describe at some length the chief aspects of fishery labour in connection with the more productive fisheries, we need not here refer to the calumnies that have been directed against the fisher folk, such as the accusations of laziness and their want of thrift. It will be seen in the sequel that such accusations are either entirely untrue or have been grossly exaggerated. " It is no doubt considered by some to be an easy way to wealth to prosecute the herring or white fish fisheries, and secure a harvest grown on a farm where there is no rent payable, the seed of which is sown in plenty by nature, which requires no manure to force it to maturity, and no wages for its cultivation. But it is not all gold that glitters. There are risks of life and property that are unknown to the industries which are followed on the land " *

The fisher folk, taking them all over, will compare most favourably with other classes as regards the labours of the men and the virtue of the women ; their humble homes, as a

* ' Harvest of the Sea '—third edition.

rule, are clean and tidily arranged, and in some villages a profane word is scarcely ever heard. The hospitality of the fisher folk is proverbial, and their charity, at times when a boat is wrecked, and the bread-winner of a family is drowned, is active and unbounded. In not a few of our fishing villages there may be seen in the houses of different families little boarders who have found a home with the other children of the place, their fathers having gone down in the waves on the occasion of a storm overtaking the fishing fleet and wrecking some of the boats. There is much that is heroic in these communities, and deeds of charity have many a time been done, which had they been blazoned by the press, would have excited the unbounded admiration of the people.

THE SCOTTISH HERRING FISHERS, THEIR WORK AND WAGES.

The capture of the herring, the principal fishing industry of Scotland —Money value of the herring—Scotland's share of the herring wealth enormous—Number of persons connected with the herring fishing— The curer the chief agent in the organisation of the fishery—Constitution of the herring fishery of Scotland—The fishing contracts— Bargaining—Extent of the netting used in the capture of the herring—Work of the fishery described—The gutters—The "hired hands"—Incidental phases of the fishing for the herring —The sprat fishery.

THE capture of the herring may be set down as the principal fishing industry of Scotland. The herring harvest gives employment, at certain seasons, to the whole fishing population, and the labour involved in the capture of that abounding fish is very much greater than most persons would think. Although the herring fishery is carried on at some place or another all the year round, we shall not visit the varied seats of that particular industry, but confine ourselves to one of those great centres which has become a rendezvous for the fishing boats of many smaller localities.

The wealth derived from the herring is enormous, the total value of these fish which are captured by boats of the United Kingdom has been set down at the handsome figure of about three millions sterling. Scotland long ago succeeded Holland as the seat of the "great fishery," and it has been calculated that more than 150,000 persons derive some portion at least of their means of living from "the herring," the capture and cure of which in many places of the United Kingdom, and also in Ireland, is a long established feature of fishery economy.

The chief agent in the organisation of this very onerous industry is known in Scottish fishing ports as "the curer," two-thirds of the herring which are caught by boats fishing from Scottish ports, being ultimately sold as *cured* herrings, the other third finding its way to market—by means of industrious "buyers" who are now to be found at every fishing port—as "fresh herrings." Herring commerce is still to a large extent centred in the curer, who finds the materials necessary for the cure, and engages persons to superintend the different processes which are incidental to its progress. Some curers carry on a really gigantic business, engaging to accept the fish which are caught by several hundred boats, besides buying, as occasion offers, from boats fishing on their own account. It is necessary to state this in order to show such features of the business as relate to the earnings of the fishermen employed, many of whom receive but a scanty share of the large sums, which at times are paid for the fish. It has to be said generally of the herring fishery as regards the remuneration of the larger number of those engaged in it, that it partakes greatly of the nature of a lottery, in which some few fortunate individuals secure most of the prizes, leaving the blanks to the majority of those who participate in the enterprise.

Before proceeding to give details of the really hard labour involved in catching the fish, it will be as well to describe in a few sentences the constitution of the fishery. We will assume then that Mr. Peterkin, of Wick—there is probably no such person, but we shall assume that there is—has set up business as a curer, has become the tenant of a space of ground, has erected upon it a cooperage, and has imported any quantity of barrel wood, and purchased salt with which to pickle the herrings, as well as numerous miscellaneous stores likely to prove useful in the course of the season, including dye-stuff for nets, nets, sails, oars and whisky. The curer is of course a man of some means; if not the possessor of ready money himself he is able, we shall suppose, to obtain credit at one or other of the local banks ("cash credits" on good security being a leading feature of the Scottish banking system). Every curer must have money at command, as in numerous instances many of his payments have to be made long before he can realise the goods which he deals in. As a matter of fact, the curer often bargains for his herrings months before he can obtain them—long indeed before it can be known whether or not there will be any herrings to capture ; and part of the bargain made by the fishers is a stipulation for so much ready money—known in fishing circles as "bounty"—in addition to the sum per barrel (or *cran*, which is a measure capable of containing 36 gallons of fish) which he binds himself to pay for the herring, and perquisites of various kinds which he agrees to provide, such perhaps as cutch with which to *bark*, or dye the nets, drying-ground for the nets, and a quantity of tea, coffee or ardent spirits, although whisky, as has been already stated, is not nowadays so much in demand as it used to be, in consequence of the more temperate habits of the men. The curer usually contracts with each boat-master to supply him with two hundred barrels of herrings, if he can capture so many ; and a curer may have twenty or a hundred boats fishing for him, according to the amount of capital at his command, and the means he may possess of disposing of the cured herrings. The striking of a bargain between the boatmaster—or, as we had

better call him, the skipper—is often a rather tough affair ;
all parties, as we may say, are working in the dark ; neither
of the men who are engaged in the arrangement can tell
how next year's markets will formulate—if herrings prove
to be scarce, then prices will be high ; if, on the contrary,
there occurs a glut of fish, prices will fall at once to a
probably unprofitable figure.

These are all features of the coming fishery which require
to be taken into account ; and, moreover, although the curer
arranges for the supplying of two hundred barrels of fish
by each of the boats fishing for him, he is not usually provided with a stock of salt sufficient to cure that quantity,
he does not perhaps calculate that he will receive on the
average more from each of his boats than from eighty to one
hundred and twenty barrels—" crans " are however what are
bargained for, but we prefer to use the word barrel, as the
sale of the cured fish takes place in barrels.   Generally bargains are struck on the figures of previous years, the curer
trying as well as he is able to forecast the features of the
season, and to picture in his mind's eye the fortunes of
" the fishery."   If all the fish bargained for were to be
caught, the chances are that the curer would be " caught "
as well ; his stock of salt would rapidly run out, and his
supply of barrels prove utterly inadequate, as has not
infrequently proved to be the case during previous seasons
when a glut of fish has occurred.   Besides these *désagrémens*,
his gutters would not in all probability be able to overtake
the necessary work, and so a large proportion of the fish
captured would in a sense be wasted, as to obtain the best
official brand, it is absolutely necessary that the herrings be
cured on the day they are caught.

Curers are often blamed for their desire to " force
business " in connection with the herring fishery ; and

probably in the case of speculative curers the blame is in many instances deserved ; and whenever misfortune overtakes a fishing community the curer is blamed as being in some way the cause of it. Young men anxious to become owners of a boat and to engage in the fishing on their own account, instead of continuing as the hired servants of other boatmasters, are often able to indulge their ambition by the aid of a speculative curer, who will supply all that is required—boat and fishing-gear complete—on credit entirely, or partly for cash, and partly on credit as may be agreed upon, but not of course without some distinct advantage to himself in connection with such a speculative transaction. He will charge a higher price for the boat and its gear, and he will make a harder bargain with the owners for the produce of their fishings. Such transactions occasionally terminate favourably for all connected with them ; a series of fortunate seasons enables the buyer of the boat to pay off his debt and to become a free fisher, at liberty to dispose of the proceeds of his industry to whomsoever he pleases. This will not appear in the least improbable when it is taken into consideration that by one evening's work a boat's crew may draw from the water a hundred pounds' worth of herring. On the other hand, the owners of a vessel may work hard for a whole season, and scarcely obtain a larger sum than will pay the wages or shares of those hired to assist them. It is not to be expected that the industry of herring fishing will be barren of such incidents, so long as young men are ambitious and curers are willing to speculate. The cost of a boat and a suite of nets, it may be added, is much greater than it used to be ; herring boats are of a larger build now, most of them being decked or half-decked vessels, in place of the open yawls that were in almost universal use for the shore herring fishery twenty years ago.

The herring boats of the period, with all their fittings, will cost on the average about £270, whilst nets will cost about £3 each.

When the bargain has been made, the labour of fishing begins at the proper season, the fishing on the Scottish coasts being at its height in the month of August. The fishing-boats engaged in the herring fishery are frequently being improved, and will doubtless some day be much better than even the best of them are at present, far ahead as these are of the old "Clinker" Leith built boats once so much in favour.* As has been hinted, many of the boats are "family concerns," and, that being so, come to be worn out in time, the money earned being all required for the use of those dependent on the vessel, and as repairs are not always made when necessary, the boat in due time becomes unfit for the work incidental to the herring fishery, and in the end is laid up a sheer hulk quite useless for any purpose whatever. A number of the boats engaged in the herring fishery are still the open

---

* As to the superiority of large boats over small ones, we have gleaned the following information from a report of the Scottish fishery board, in which the fishery officer at Eyemouth states that those crews who fished from large decked boats with some amount of perseverance, made from £200 to £300 for the season, whilst the crews of adjacent ports were not fortunate, not being so well prepared. In a few instances, sums of from £500 to £700 were earned by the decked boats. Open boats with inferior netting made only from £60 to £120. In a few boats homing pigeons are carried : they are let off as soon as the catch is determined, to let the curer know what number of barrels he may calculate upon. One drawback in connection with the use of the larger boats is that, should they be becalmed the herrings with which they are laden will not be received in time for the cure. Steam tugs should, in such cases, be kept in readiness to bring in the boats, till the time comes when steam vessels are regularly employed in the fishery. This, we believe, is now being done.

clinker-built boats that have been so long in use , they are usually manned by four persons in addition to the skipper, who may be either sole or part owner, and all on board find plenty of work to do on each evening of the fishery, for although the boat is provided with a large shoulder-of-mutton sail, it often enough happens that the oars have to be resorted to in order to reach the supposed haunts of the fish, and always as a general practice when the nets are being "shot"—that is, paid overboard. During late years the labour of herring-fishing has been greatly augmented by the increased quantity of netting which is thought to be necessary as compared with the net power employed twenty-five or thirty years ago. Some very interesting details regarding the nets used by the herring fleet were collected and published by the Commissioners who inquired into the condition of the Scottish herring-fisheries six years ago. As giving some idea of the labour which the nightly distribution of the netting entails, we beg to lay before our readers the following summary of figures, relating to the increase of net power, and the revolution which has been caused by the substitution of finely-woven cotton for hemp nets —

Twenty years ago a boat carried 24 nets made of hemp, each net forty yards long, with 28 or 29 meshes to the yard, 10 to 12 score meshes deep, and weighing 25 lbs. Each boat carries now 50 to 60 nets made of cotton, each net 60 yards long, with 35 meshes to the yard, 18 score meshes deep, and weighing 12 to 14 lbs A boat, in other words, used to carry 960 yards of netting ; it now carries 3,300 yards. The nets used to be about six or seven yards, they are now over ten yards deep. They used to present a catching surface of 3000 square yards ; they now present a catching surface of 33,000 square yards.

Such is the formidable instrument of fishing which the crews of the herring boats have to handle on each night they are at sea. The nets of the fleet of herring boats which on some nights may be found fishing off the coast of Aberdeenshire could reach six times across the North Sea, and in instances the suite of netting which is cast overboard from one boat will extend two miles in length. The herring-boats usually commence to leave the harbours for their fishing stations early in the afternoon ; if there should be a favouring breeze they hoist their sail, and reap the advantage of a speedy run to the spot selected, which however is not always the place where they find the fish Often enough a boat proceeds to fish at a place that may be from thirty to forty miles distant from the port of rendezvous, and it is all a matter of luck whether or not the men hit upon the shoal. The work of shooting the nets usually begins at sunset : the mast is struck, and, two men taking the oars, the boat is moved slowly across the tide ; the skipper of course keeps possession of the helm, having first of all selected his theatre of operations ; the remaining two men of the crew have the duty of throwing over the nets into the sea. As the writer is well able to testify, having more than once personally taken part in the work, it is a laborious process, and requires some care, occupying a considerable time, so that when it is concluded the men are ready for a little refreshment and a few hours' rest. They partake of a frugal supper, and in some boats the skipper will ask the men to join him in singing a hymn, and he may perhaps offer up a simple prayer, asking the blessing of God on his enterprise. Ordinarily the men who have been working at the oars, as well as their fellow-labourers

C

at the paying-over of the nets, speedily fall asleep, and enjoy an hour or two of "blessed rest."

But the skipper, who may himself be either the owner of the boat or hold a share in it, seldom sleeps ; he is all too anxious about the venture, and sits throughout the silent watches of the night speculating on the number of "crans" of herring that he may see brought into the boat when the hour of hauling in the nets arrives. Before that time however his curiosity as to the good or bad fortune of the night may have culminated in a desire to see whether his nets have been so fortunate as to hit the shoal, and so he pulls in a few yards of the floating fabric, to see if there be fish ; or mayhap he may be tempted to examine the nets attached to a neighbouring boat, to find out what degree of fortune has attended it. Sometimes it happens that after the nets have been shot, and the boat has been drifting with the tide for an hour or two, there are no signs of the shoal having been hit upon, so that a new departure becomes necessary, and the whole of the labour has to be incurred a second time ; the nets have to be hauled on board, the boat rowed to another pitch, where the huge fabric of capture is again cast into the waters in search of prey : again the men lay themselves down to their rest ; again the boat, with the watchful skipper at the helm, floats about for an hour of two, when comes the final test of the night's fortunes. Let us assume that success has at length been achieved, and that the fifty or sixty barrels of fish which have been enmeshed adds to the labour of the enterprise. Two miles length of netting, often enough heavily laden with newly-caught herrings, have to be hauled on board, the fish have to be shaken or picked from the meshes, and the boat, wind or no wind, has to make its

way home to port in order that the curer may obtain
possession of the cargo. Many a time and oft the poor
men have, on their way back to their harbour, to row a
good part of the way; and when the sea is lumpy and
the boat laden with fish—a delightful burden in the eyes
of its owners—the toil is severe. Nor is the labour over
when the port is reached, for then begins a new duty—
the fish have to be landed, and it is the work of the crew
to carry them to the curing stances, which may be at a
considerable distance from the place in the harbour where
the boat has found a berth. After the fish have been
duly consigned to the charge of the coopers, the nets
have then to be hoisted ashore and sent off in a cart to the
drying ground ; and not till all these duties have been duly
accomplished may captain and crew seek repose.

And thus the toilsome work of the herring-fishers goes
on day after day; on some happy occasions they may
be so fortunate as to fall in with the shoal a few miles from
the shore, and fill their nets with such speed as to enable
them to return before breakfast-time, and so obtain a few
hours of welcome rest; or, on the contrary, they may not
find their finny prey till they are far, far at sea ; and not
infrequently, before their labour can be brought to a close,
a fierce storm may break on the waters, causing the men to
hurry to a place of refuge, if they can find one, in order
to save their lives and property, a feat which cannot
always be accomplished. Many a fishing boat on such
occasions is swamped by the angry waters, and many a
gallant husband and good father perishes whilst at the
post of duty. The public are not unfamiliar with stories
of the dread disasters which occasionally overtake the
hardy fishermen of our coasts, although in Scotland it
is happily the case that the death rate from such causes

is considerably less than it is elsewhere, the hereditary
Scottish fishers being an anxious and careful body of men.

But although the men who caught the fish are in bed
asleep the industrial drama of the herring cure still goes
on ; as the boats reach the harbour a new phase of work
begins. As has been stated, the greater portion of the
herring taken are cured, which involves their being gutted
and salted as well as being packed in barrels. These
processes are all organised by the curer and his confidential
assistant, the head cooper ; the women who are entrusted
with the disagreeable work of eviscerating the fish perform their part with great celerity, and will go on working
for several hours in the most active way. They are paid
according to the tale of work they do, which is a great
incitement to industry. A woman has been timed to gut
two dozen herrings in a minute, so that she can fill a
barrel in the course of about thirty-five minutes. When
it is considered that over a million barrels of herrings are
cured in Scotland every year, and that each barrel contains
over seven hundred and fifty fish, it will be apparent that the
females engaged in the work of evisceration have plenty of
work cut out for them, seeing that the season on the north-
east coast of Scotland, where most of the herrings are cured,
only lasts for about eight weeks. We do not know any
other kind of labour for women that could be classed with
the curing of herrings, and we dare say it would be rather
difficult to find females in inland places who would consent
to work at the herring troughs. The rate of payment for
this kind of work used to be at the rate of fourpence for
each barrel of herring filled with the gutted fish ; and
hundreds of persons fishermen's widows and others were
very glad of the work, so that they might earn a few pounds
during the course of the fishery. At such times as there is

a large fishing—"a glut of herrings"—active gutters are at a premium, whilst the wages paid for the work are increased ; an expert party of six women will make up over one hundred and thirty barrels in a long day.

It may be as well, before going farther, to state more definitely than has been done the figures pertaining to the herring fishery, so far as wages and allowances are concerned. Premising that the terms agreed upon may not be alike in any two places, it may here be chronicled, that agreements at the rate of a pound per cran for the tale of two hundred crans with a bounty of perhaps thirty or forty pounds, and in some instances fifty pounds, have this season (1883) been entered into ; various perquisites of the kind already indicated being also included in the bargain. Many of the hired men now prefer to share in the luck of the fishery and take their chance of payment at a certain rate per cran rather than accept fixed wages : say one shilling, or two shillings per cran, as the case may be, as also a fixed sum by way of bounty, as well as other advantages of various kinds. The terms made by the hired men depend, of course, a good deal on the state of the labour market ; when a new centre of herring fishing industry arises, or an old one develops itself, as is the case in Shetland, both men and women flock to it in the hope of obtaining better terms than would be offered them at older established fisheries. These men are now much better paid than they used to be some thirty years ago, when, for the whole period of "the fishing," a five-pound note would perhaps be their utmost reward. These "hired men," it should be stated, are many of them mere labourers, and not expert fishers— they are a mixture of the small farmer, the village mechanic, and the sailor, glad enough to turn out in the herring season, the best that can be said of most of them is that they are hardy and willing labourers, anxious to earn a few pounds when "siller is a-going."

As to the women, the Fraserburgh correspondent of the *Scotsman* newspaper recently stated that, "Women, to work as gutters, are in great demand, and the wages offered them are quite unprecedented. The rates of arles for the eight weeks' work run from £1 10s. to £5 each, besides 8d. per barrel gutted and packed by the crew. It is only a few years since a woman considered herself highly paid if she got 5s of arles. A number of women belonging to the town have gone to Shetland this season, and the present competition is, no doubt, due to that."

Mr. James Wilson's description (*Voyage Round the Coast of Scotland,* 1842) of the work of gutting is graphic : "though the gutters are not a few of them good-looking creatures, yet the appearance of the general mass after they have worked an hour or two, beggars all description. Their hands, their necks, their busts, their

'Dreadful faces throng'd, and fiery arms'

every bit about them fore and aft, are spotted and be-sprinkled with little scarlet clots of gills and guts, or as Southey says of the war horse of Don Roderick, after the last and fatal fight—

'Their flanks incarnadined,
Their poitral smeared with blood.'

Bloody and all begrimed with slime the gutter stands up with knife in hand, or stoops her horrid head 'with scaly armour bright,' and plunging her bare and brawny arms again into the trough, scatters her gills and guts, as if no bowels of compassion existed any more on this terraqueous globe. . . . Towards evening they carefully wash their faces, arms and legs, and slip on again their better garments. Thus they never appear except around the gutting

board in otherwise than trim array. Indeed, many of the
most magnificently fine females, whom we saw standing at
respectable doors, or looking out of decent windows, or
going sedately about their evening occupations from shop
to shop, had been assiduously engaged in gutting all day
long."

On some one or two days during every season's fishing,
at Wick and other important herring ports—Fraserburgh
and Peterhead are now rather before Wick as centres of
the fishery—the delivery of fish from, perhaps, five in the
morning till four o'clock in the afternoon will be so
incessant and in such large quantities that the whole
industrial resources and activity of the place will be called
into requisition, as it is of the utmost importance that the
herrings landed should be cured by set of sun, so as to
secure the best brand. The close of a successful herring
fishing season is always marked in Scotland by the great
number of marriages which take place ; in many of the
smaller fishing ports the weddings of the young people
depend on the fishery. If it should prove a failure, marriages
are postponed in consequence, and men and women agree
to wait for more prosperous times. We have not the means
of determining exactly how many persons are employed
throughout Scotland in the capture of the herring only,
but, taking men and boys together, there will probably be
not less than fifty thousand persons, whilst the amount of
capital sunk in boats, fishing-gear, and the materials of the
cure will probably not be less than a million sterling.
According to an official document which we have examined
there were over 14,000 fishing vessels of all kinds in
Scotland in the year 1881, the larger number of them being
employed in the shore fishery for herrings. Some fishermen make it their business to fish for the herring all the

year round, and these, as the saying is, "follow the fish" from the far-away seas of Scotland to Yarmouth, and scarcely ever know an idle day. Wherever the herrings make their appearance the Scottish boats, with their hardy and industrious crews, are sure to be participating in the work of capture, whether at Cullercoats, Holy Island, the Isle of Man, or Yarmouth.

We have, so far, only endeavoured to show the round of labour incidental to the chief herring fishery of the year— there are winter herring fisheries in Scotland as well, some of which are very successful, but the great outlet for all persons interested in "the herring" is, of course, the fisheries of the autumn season. Then a large number of persons who do not fish all the year round, try to earn "an orra pound or maybe twa" by assisting, at what is at that season an almost universal industry; cobblers lay down their lapstones, gardeners put aside their spades, and turn out with some one or other of the boats, in the hope of sharing in the bounty of the waters. At the chief herring ports a large number of persons other than the usual population find employment; an influx of men and women from the Highlands and Islands is one of the features of the fishing season. The hawking of fresh herrings from such places as Montrose, Peterhead, and Berwick or Eyemouth, also affords employment to a considerable number of persons, so that the bustle incidental to a herring port in the brief time devoted to the capture of the fish produces an exciting change in some usually quiet enough fishing communities. It is evident, too, that a sum of two and a half millions sterling, which it has been calculated should in recent years be about the value of the herrings caught in Scotland will cover a large series of distributions. The capture of the sprat in its season (a toothsome fish), for which there is always a great demand, would prove a remunerative winter fishery, were it not for the high rates of freight charged for its conveyance to the seats of population where it is consumed. As a profit cannot be made on the consignments, sprat-fishing is for a time somewhat in abeyance.

We have dwelt at some length on the industrial phases of the Scottish herring fishery, because it is of great moment as a food resource, likewise as an outlet for the employment of capital, in the catching and curing of the fish— as well as in the building of boats, the making of barrels, the weaving of sails and the making of nets. In the course of the year, at one place or another, the herring fishery of Scotland yields employment more or less remunerative to the whole of the fishing population of that country— hence its importance as compared with places where the capture of the herring only forms a portion of the general round of fishery work.

THE FISHERS OF YARMOUTH.

Herring fishing on the English coasts—Herring catch at Yarmouth
—Size of vessels and modes of work—Mode of paying the crew
—Yarmouth bloaters and kippers—Scottish boats at Yarmouth—
Curing processes.

WE do not propose to follow the herring-fishers to every
place where there is a rendezvous for their boats—in other
words, a seat of the fishery. The labour attendant on the
Scottish system of drift-net fishing has been detailed in the
preceding pages ; but in Scotland, especially in Lochfyne,
another mode of capturing the herring has been long in use.
We allude to " seining," or, as it is called locally, trawling.
It is not so laborious as the drift-net mode of fishing, and
seems a suitable mode of taking the herring in such waters
as Lochfyne. In some years seining has proved very
remunerative to the men, in consequence of the fish being
plentiful ; but there, as elsewhere, the fishing is irregular, and
no one can say how he has fared till the end of the season,
a few lucky hauls on one or two days of the fishing may
make all the difference between good and bad fortune.
No other modes of fishing for herrings have been adopted
in Scotland other than seining and drift-net fishing ; and, as
has been stated, the herring-fishery in Scotland is chiefly a
shore-fishery, which of course adds greatly to the toil of the
fisher folk. The practice of " yair-fishing " is now, we
think, very uncommon, but we have seen yairs, or en-
closures, in Lochbroom, into which the herrings enter and
are left high and dry by the tide. There are a few decked

boats in connection with the Scottish herring-fishery which
have accommodation on board for carrying on the cure,
but the leisurely labour on these vessels is less onerous
than that of the shore-fisheries, where the work goes on
at a ding-dong rate from sunrise to sunset, for the sake
of securing the best brand to the greatest possible number
of barrels.

There is herring-fishing in abundance on the coast of
Northumberland, and the Isle of Man herring-fishing in
some seasons is very productive; but we shall now take
up our station for a brief period at Yarmouth, which is
an important seat of fishing industry, and has acquired
a great name for the extent of its commerce in cured
herrings. The fish of that kind brought into the port
of Yarmouth are not, however, cured as in Scotland, the
herrings being mostly manipulated as bloaters and reds.
According to some statistics published by Mr. De Caux,
" during the last thirteen years the grand total of herrings
delivered at Great Yarmouth has been at least 210,000
lasts, or the marvellous quantity of 2,772,000,000 of herrings." But a still better idea is conveyed of the magnitude
of the fishery work which is brought to a focus at Yarmouth
by a knowledge of the fact that during every season, on an
average, the mere operation of counting the herrings landed
at the fish-wharf costs upwards of £2,200, while for simply
helping to lift the herrings from the ground on to the carts
which convey them from the wharf to the various curing-
houses, or to the railway-stations, no less a sum than £370
is paid. The number of fishers from all places congregated
at Yarmouth during the herring-season will not, we think, be
less than 12,500. At least a thousand boats went out day by
day from Yarmouth in search of the herring in 1882. The
crews are paid according to the number of herrings which

they capture. The vessels engaged in the fishery are larger and better furnished than the usual run of Scottish herring-boats. This is necessary, because they carry a crew of from ten to thirteen persons, and remain out fishing a night or two. The boats are full-decked, have two, and sometimes three, masts, and are strongly built, so as to stand the stress of weather. These vessels carry each a suite of 100 nets, each net being 48 feet long by 30 feet deep.

The labour involved on board of these boats is consider-able. The men shoot the nets and haul them in oftener than once in the course of the night—the fishing commencing at sunset. The mode of work is well-planned throughout, every man having his allotted duty to perform ; one person looks after the corks and floats, another, with an assistant, pays out the netting, whilst another has charge of the warp-rope to which the nets are fixed. After being ex-amined about every two hours, when it is thought a suffi-cient number of fish have struck, the nets are hauled on board by means of the steam-driven capstan, now gene-rally used by North Sea boats, and being passed over a horizontal pole, the herrings are "shook out," falling into the hold : each net as it is emptied being carefully stowed away in its appointed place, to be ready for use when the time arrives to make another shot ; in fact, the discipline in these herring vessels is about as exacting as on board a man-of-war. When the herrings are got on board there is still more work to accomplish : they have to be "roused" with salt, and, after that operation has been carefully performed, have to be packed carefully away in the hold ; and, as on some occasions the nets are full of fish, there is plenty of work for all hands.

It is quite certain that the hardy fishers of Yarmouth do not eat the bread of idleness in the times of herring-fishing, which lasts, for winter fish, from the beginning of October to the end of November. It is perhaps almost unnecessary to say that the boats require to proceed cautiously while engaged in the operation of fishing; there is a large fleet employed in the work, and if the men were careless there might occur a series of en- tanglements of the nets that could not fail to be irrita- ting, and probably result in the partial loss of the fish taken. On this head, Mitchell tells us in his work on ' The Herring,' that the greatest precaution is taken to prevent the nets from mixing. " No fishing vessel," he says, " anchors except during the day, when the nets are not out, or unless the weather is so calm at night as to prevent the possibility of shooting the nets ; and during the night each vessel has a lantern at the bow, upon a pole sufficiently elevated to be seen at the distance of five miles " Should, for instance, a decided change of wind occur after the nets are shot, the whole business must be gone over again— the nets have to be hauled in and re-shot, to prevent the terrible confusion and loss that might result Much fatigu- ing work is involved on such occasions, and the crews are sometimes very tired. As has been already stated, the fishermen of Yarmouth are paid by results ; the curers arrange at the beginning of the season with their own crews to pay them a fixed price for every boat-load they bring in. This is instead of paying a regular sum of money monthly as wages ; and it induces the men to do their best, as a considerable catch of fish is necessary to enable the curers to pay the expenses of their vessels and establishments before they can make any profit.*

As is well known, a considerable portion of the herrings which are brought ashore at Yarmouth are cured in a

* ' Deep Sea Fishing and Fishing Boats,' by Holdsworth.

peculiar fashion, which industry employs many hands at fair
wages. The "Yarmouth bloater" is known all over the
world. The story of the "invention," or rather discovery,
of this mode of cure has been told by Mr. De Caux, in his
little work on 'The Herring and the Herring Fishery.'
We venture to abridge it for the information of our readers,
without, however, entering into any details of the process of the cure ; suffice it to say that a bloater is a fresh
herring slightly salted and smoked, but not gutted ; it will
not keep beyond three or four days, and should therefore be eaten promptly. The mode of making bloaters
was discovered by Mr. Bishop, a herring-curer of Yarmouth,
about the year 1835, but the precise date at which it took
place is unknown. The following account of the discovery is, we believe, correct : " One night, after his
fish-house hands had left the place, Mr. Bishop found
a small quantity of a prime parcel of fresh herrings which
he thought had by some mischance been overlooked.
To prevent the fish from being spoiled, he sprinkled
them with salt, spitted them, and then hung them up in
a 'smoke house,' in which oak billet was then being
burned ; and the next morning he was both astonished and
delighted at their appearance, as well as with their aroma
and flavour. Henceforth he made the cure of bloaters a
special pursuit, and, as other curers speedily followed his
example, in a very short time the 'Yarmouth bloater'
became known far and wide." "Newcastle kippers" denote
another mode of curing the herring, which affords employment to a large number of the women folk of Yarmouth.
This branch of the fishery business we are told was introduced by Mr. John Woodger, formerly of Newcastle ; and the
late Mr Buckland learned that as many as 1500 lasts of
herrings were prepared in this manner (13,200 fish to the

last). The first samples of these kippers were prepared
for public sale in 1846, and now herrings cured in that style
have a firm hold of the market.

In the year 1881 the take of herrings by the Yarmouth boats amounted, we are told, to 16,725 lasts, or
220,770,000 individual herrings. As to the curing processes in vogue at Yarmouth, it may be stated here that
they vary according to the future of the fish. Bloaters
are not "gypped" (i.e. gutted), but other kinds of cured
fish are, just as in Scotland. The "curing works" at
Yarmouth are well worthy of being visited when the
herrings are on hand. They are perfect hives of industry.
There are registered at the port of Great Yarmouth 621
vessels of all kinds, of 15 tons and upwards, and these
boats employ 5160 hands on board ; there are besides a
large number of boats under 15 tons that rendezvous at the same port—there are, for instance, 300
boats from various ports of Scotland, that come south
to the herring fishery ; there are, including shrimpers,
150 other vessels, as well as 120 smacks, from Gorleston.

The Scottish boats which fish at Yarmouth, it may be
stated, are smaller than the local vessels, and carry suites
of finer netting. They fish for the fresh herring trade, and
run into port with their catch for immediate sale. It is
interesting to note that, if the number of herrings recorded
above were to bring one halfpenny each to their captors,
the sum would amount to £459,937. The herring fishery
only occupies a small portion of the time of the Yarmouth
fishermen ; how the remainder of their time is occupied
will be seen by consulting another division of this work
—THE FISHERS OF THE GREAT NORTH SEA.

THE CORNWALL PILCHARD CATCHERS.

Importance of the pilchard—Catching pilchards by the seine net—
Earnings of the pilchard-catchers—Cure of the fish—"The Pope
and pilchards"—The pilchard Harvest—Drift-net fishing by
Cornwall boats.

THE pilchard is an important member of the herring
family, the capture of which may be said to form the staple
fishing industry of the coast of Cornwall, and it may be
said of the Cornish fisher folk that they greatly resemble
the fisher people of Scotland, inasmuch as they are hereditary fishers, and conduct their business much in the same
way as many of the Scottish fishermen conduct theirs.
The boats in many instances are family concerns, and the
profits made are divided in equitable proportions among
the crew.   These fish are in some seasons more abundant
than others, and are anxiously watched for and industriously
fished when found   It is not our cue in the present work
to deal with the natural history of the pilchard, but we may
perhaps be allowed to say that the circumstance of the fish
frequently coming in shore in large bodies—"schulls" these
bodies are called in Cornwall—affords an opportunity to
the most stay-at-home fisherman to participate in the work
of capture.   This coming in of the fish to the bays has
given rise to one of the modes of capture, namely, that
mode which is carried on by means of the seine net, and
which has been so successfully imitated by the herring
fishermen of Lochfyne in Scotland. It may be explained,
however, that the seine or sean net, either as used in Corn-

wall or in some modified form, is also used in various other fisheries than those for members of the herring family; in fact it is used occasionally for the taking of all sorts of fish, and not for one fish in particular. When conducted in that way seining is denominated "blind fishing." We may briefly describe here the labours undergone by the fishermen of Cornwall in connection with the working of a seine net, the use of which is so to enclose the fish of a shoal as to prevent their escape, and keep them alive till the men and women can carry them ashore to the curing houses.

The industry of pilchard catching by means of the seine net is pretty well organised, as may be seen in the bay of St Ives in the months of September, October and November, with its many picturesque developments this mode of pilchard capture is well worth watching; when a shoal has been successfully surrounded by the nets, a period of great activity at once ensues, the work accomplished during which speedily makes up for many days of enforced idleness. About the period when the fish may be expected to come inland, patrols are appointed to parade the high places of the coast, and give notice, by means of preconcerted signals, of the approach of the pilchards. These persons are designated "huers," and are chosen for their qualities of quick-sightedness and general activity. These sentinels of the Cornwall pilchard fisheries take each a spell of duty of three hours' duration, there being two men to each look-out station They used to signal to the fishermen by means of a branch held in their hand; but on the St. Ives stations there is a staff on which is fixed a movable ball of a white colour, by means of which directions are telegraphed to the boats to indicate the locality of the shoal. These men who raise the hue and cry on the approach of the fish have fixed wages for the period they are at work, of £3 per month, and a perquisite besides of every hundredth hogshead of the fish captured by the boats which they serve. The wages or remuneration of the fishermen employed in the same boats is at the rate of 45s. per month, one-ninth part of the fish caught being also their property. There are also men called "blowsers," whose duty it is to land the fish and carry them to the curing cellars—their pay is arranged in proportion to the catch of fish. The wages in "kind" are at once paid, the ninth part of the fish being promptly taken possession of and divided among those entitled to them. According to Mr. Thomas Couch: "The crew of a sean consists of eighteen men, and commonly a boy. The wages of the ordinary seaner have varied from eight to twelve shillings a week ; the men who actually shoot the sean have a shilling a week extra, while the master-seaner's pay is a guinea, with a gratuity on each hundred hogsheads which he is so fortunate as to catch ; besides which the crew are in common entitled to a third part of the fish sold fresh, and a fourth of that which is exported ; in some places not even paying for the casks in which they are packed."

As there are 250 "concerns" (seines) in working order at St Ives, it is obvious that they cannot all be at work at the same time, and it has therefore been wisely arranged among the proprietors that each shall take his turn at the fish, according to a scheme laid down to which all have agreed. The seines can only be worked from half-a-dozen positions, and, so that there may be fair play, all the seines are registered, individual owners agreeing among themselves to work on the co-operative system ; and therefore at the beginning of each season a uniform plan of operations is agreed upon at a meeting of the seine owners, whereby each attains a turn or two turns, according to capacity, some concerns being much larger than others.

The pilchards are cured in a particular manner, and the cure affords plenty of work while it is in progress, those engaged in it being chiefly the women of the place, who also cure at home their husbands' share of the fish for family use ; and these, with the accompaniment of potatoes, form a large portion of their daily food. The pilchards are exported for the behoof of foreign countries, where they are much esteemed. " The Pope and Pilchards " used to be a favourite toast in some parts of Cornwall.

As showing the continued work which results from a successful catch, it may be mentioned that as many as thirteen million pilchards have been enclosed in one seine. The advantage of using such nets is, that the fish, being securely tucked within the seine by means of an additional net, may be kept alive till the cure of the whole lot can be undertaken and completed, which is accomplished at leisure, so to put the case, although the people are certainly busy enough whilst any of the work remains to be accomplished The oil which exudes from the pilchards while they are being cured is valuable, and is used chiefly by curriers in the preparation of some kinds of leather ; the yield of oil is about two gallons per hogshead. As we have already said, the pilchard harvest fluctuates very much ; the number of fish mentioned above is the largest ever taken at one operation. In the year 1881 the quantity of cured pilchards exported was close upon 14,000 hogsheads, and the price per hogshead to the curers averaged about 58s.—in one year as many as 45,000 hogsheads have been cured. But, as in the Scottish herring fishery, there is also a large consumption in Cornwall and other counties during the

D 2

season of "fresh" pilchards, whilst there is likewise a local sale of cured fish.

Having said so much about the seine nets, we may now refer to the drift-net fishing, which forms a prominent feature of Cornwall industry. We do not know the exact number of the fishing population that find employment in Cornwall in connection with the pilchard, mackerel, and general fisheries, but there are 624 boats of all sizes, valued at £368,000. Some account of the drift-net fishing of Cornwall, so far as its industrial aspects are concerned, is contained in a recent official report of an inquiry, and from that blue book we are indebted for the materials of the following summary. On the drift-net fishery boats are employed varying in size from half-decked luggers of 15 tons and 26-foot keel, engaged in the pilchard fishery, to full-decked luggers of 30 tons and 46-foot keel or more, employed in the mackerel fishery. The pilchard drivers rarely go far from shore, and always return to their port within 24 hours. Mackerel drivers follow their fish into the deep sea, and sometimes fish more than 30 leagues from the nearest land ; and as these are the boats principally affected by the inquiry referred to above, the remainder of this memorandum must be read as referring to them. Each of their voyages is usually completed within 24 hours when on the home fishery ; but sometimes, when several boats are in concert, many remain out for a week at a time, one of the fleet running for port each morning with the night's catch of the whole lot.

These boats are owned by individuals, and never by a company. They are manned by crews of about seven men and a boy, raised from the fishing villages from which they hail, all well known to each other, and very frequently related ;

and the owner not unusually acts as master—if he does not
a brother or a son, or some other relative, usually does.
The " boy " is almost always related to some one on board
the boat.

These boats, in the seasons, go to Plymouth, the York-
shire coasts, and the Bay of Dublin. They never go far
enough from shore to make it necessary that their masters
should know the science of navigation. Nothing is required
in a master but a knowledge of reading (so that he may
learn up the lights and work a chart) and good practical
seamanship ; and of boats on these voyages it may also be
remarked that no one has ever been lost through want of
these qualifications. The crews of these boats are never
shipped at wages ; they work on share. Each man has the
privilege of bringing on board a certain number of nets
(a " net " is a length of net varying in the different fishing
villages), and the earnings of the boat after paying her
going expenses are divided. A certain share goes for the
boat, another share for the nets, and another for the crew.
The division of these earnings takes place at entirely
uncertain periods, according to the catches of fish, but it
occurs at intervals during the fishing seasons, with a wind-
up at the end of each.

Mr. Thomas Couch in a history of Polperro, gives some
interesting particulars of the Cornwall pilchard catchers,
and describes them as a hardy race of men, often leading a
life of toil and privation, and as a body not deserving of
the hard things which have been said about them. Their
gains, despite occasional spells of hard work, never reach
any considerable sum, whilst they are at all times precarious ;
and were it not for the produce of their gardens, and their
store of salted pilchards, their fate in severe and stormy
winters would be one almost of starvation. The fishers

of the Cornwall coast, according to Mr. Couch, are remarkably shrewd and sagacious in all matters pertaining to their daily industry, but, like others of their class, they are imbued with a strong vein of superstition, and are wedded to old customs. No one can doubt the courage of the Cornish fishermen on occasions of shipwreck, or of other disasters. They have braved the dangers of the deep without the slightest prospect of being rewarded for their often successful daring, and their hospitality to those who have been shipwrecked on their iron-bound coasts is proverbial.

As regards domestic usages the fisher-folk of Cornwall lead a rather simple life, never interrupted by the celebration of the many fêtes one finds occasionally brightening the life of the same class of people in foreign countries. In his history of Polpeiro, the quaint and picturesque "little fischar toune with a peere," Mr. Couch tells us that "it was once the custom for women to take the corn to mill, see it ground, and bring home their grist, for, rightly or wrongly, millers have ever been a suspected race. Honest ones are popularly known, being distinguished by some mark or tuft of hair in the palm of the hand. Accordingly the Polperro housewives, like the two clerks of Canterbury, were accustomed for a little while—

'To go to mill and see their corn ground,'

and, as the quantity was small, to carry it home. Hence several women would be waiting for their turn at the mill, which, like the bakehouse, became a noted centre of scandal. A bit of doubtful gossip was proverbially termed 'a mill-house story.' The sale of bread, except as penny loaves, Easter and hot-cross buns, was unknown in these times."

FISHERS OF THE NORTH SEA—TRAWLERS.

The North Sea Fishermen not hereditary fishers—Severe apprenticeship
—Length of apprenticeship objected to, and should be restricted—
Bad behaviour of North Sea Fishermen—Extent of the German
Ocean—Value of the fish it yields—Trawling the chief mode of
Fishing—Fleets of Smacks—The work of Trawling—The earnings
of the trawl men.

THE fishermen of the North Sea, so far at any rate as they
hail from the chief English ports, cannot be called hereditary fishers. The fishing smacks belonging to Hull, Great
Grimsby, Yarmouth, and other ports, take apprentices from
whatever place they can obtain them, and such has been
the practice for many years, the consequence being that
these vessels are now manned by a body of fishermen who,
although they have been bred to the business, were not, as
the saying goes, "born to it." Many of the lads who are
taken as apprentices belong to families of the local labouring
classes, but a larger number are received from workhouses
and charitable institutions, and in some instances, we
believe, from reformatories. The masters of fishing vessels
have usually come through the whole round of labour incidental to all the grades of service before being appointed
to the command of their smack—the office of cook at an
early stage being one of the appointments.

It has been ascertained by inquiry that the apprenticeship
to be served on board the big fishing-boats is a severe one ;
and by several of the captains, and by the older hands on

board, the boys have been, and doubtless sometimes still are, cruelly used At whatever age a lad is bound, he continues to serve as an apprentice till he attains the age of twenty-one years ; and, as boys are frequently apprenticed who are only eleven or twelve years old, they in mary instances become heartily tired of their occupation before the expiry of their indentures. It has been suggested in consequence that indentures should not be signed for a longer period than five years Grave complaints have been made against the trawl fishers—men and boys—many of whom apparently do not conduct themselves in a reputable manner. An official inquiry has been held, and voluminous evidence taken as to the behaviour of the fishermen who proceed to the North Sea in trawling vessels, and many interesting facts have been elicited as to their modes of life and round of daily labour. One important feature of the industry has been elicited, and that is, that through the trawling service an outlet exists for the employment of a section of the population at all times rather ill to manage, and for whom it might prove somewhat difficult to obtain suitable work. The fisherman's calling on the stormy German Ocean is a healthy one, but the work is rough, and much discomfort has to be endured, occasionally spiced with incidents of supreme danger.

Although comparatively speaking a small sea, the German Ocean is a gigantic fish-pond, having a surface of more than eighty-nine millions of acres, yielding, it has been calculated, to those nations which have the privilege of dipping their nets in its waters, fish to the annual value of about twenty-five millions sterling. One hundred thousand tons of wholesome fish-food, it has been estimated, are contributed by the North Sea every year to the commissariat of London alone ; and, as may well be supposed, a large fleet

of vessels and a vast number of men and boys are employed
in the work of capture and distribution.

We propose to give a brief sketch of the chief modes of
fishing in the German Ocean, where, as a recent writer
states, "no class of men work harder, live harder, or en-
dure greater peril of their lives." What we have to describe, however, must be taken in a general sense, as we
have not sufficient space at our disposal to enter into
minute details.

" Trawling," as is generally known, is about the cheapest
way of procuring plentiful supplies of our larger table-fishes ;
no bait is required, and miraculous draughts are sometimes
obtained. Great efforts are constantly being made to improve
the vessels , at all events, they are now built on a much larger
scale than they used to be, while the introduction of a
steam-worked capstan helps to save the men from some of
the harder work which is incidental to that mode of fishing ;
and in the course of few years it is highly probable that
the North Sea fleet will also be propelled by steam. We
have steam trawlers working on various parts of the coast,
with all the appearance of success ; and the general introduction of such vessels in the North Sea is only a question
of time. That the fish should reach the market as soon
as caught, in order to be sold when thoroughly fresh and
bring the highest possible price, is a necessity of the trade ;
some of the single fishing-smacks have to run to port
with their capture as soon as it is made, in order to catch
the buyers who are waiting. If they were screws instead of
sailing vessels it is obvious enough they would be able
to make speedier voyages than they can make with every
stitch of the canvas they can carry set to catch the favouring breeze. The fishing-places, it may be stated, lie far out

in the North Sea, so that the distance to be traversed is considerable before the Great and Little Silver Pits, the Well Banks or Rodney Gut can be reached.

Most of the trawlers work in fleets, each under the command of an admiral, who by means of signals directs the routine of the fishery.

The nightly round of trawl work throughout the fleet is pretty much as follows : at sunset, as a rule, as soon as the signal is given, the work of trawling begins by the net being let overboard. It is a gigantic chamber of horrors : for the fish, when once engulfed within its capacious maw, cannot easily escape, while all that are captured are kept—great and small, prime and offal, a circumstance which, we may be allowed to state in passing, is much to be regretted, as the smaller fishes ought to be allowed to escape. The heaving of this gigantic net overboard is of course a comparatively easy matter ; not so the getting of it on board. When the trawl has been placed the men partake of supper ; and the crew, except one man, go to sleep for a few hours, till the signal is given to begin work. It is usually about eleven o'clock when the admiral sends up a rocket to announce that the nets of the fleet must be once more got on board. This is labour of an exhausting kind. The writer has known three hours elapse before the ponderous machine has been got on board all right, the men working away with all their power of will and strength of muscle. The trawl, as soon as it is hoisted on deck, is emptied of its piscine riches, which on some occasions, when fortune has been more than usually favourable, make a formidable display of fine fish ; but the fishermen have no time to expend in admiration   Many a naturalist however would really enjoy the scene, and be delighted with the crowd of curious creatures of quaint

forms that are struggling for their lives. The first operation that the men perform is to assort or classify the fish
into "prime" and "offal," which are the two classes
known in the markets, although why haddocks and some
other really good fish should be classified as offal is
not easy to tell. Anything that is absolutely worthless is
at once thrown overboard ; but all the cruel dog-fish, which in
some seasons are wondrously plentiful, are carefully killed,
they "die game" as the fishermen tell us, unless when
"settled at once," by a strong blow on the head, which is
seemingly the most vulnerable part of all fish. Such fish
as turbot and brill live a long time out of water, but soles
die quickly ; it is astonishing however what a strength
of vitality is exhibited by the smaller flat fish—which
flop about for hours after they have been captured

After a brief time elapses, the trawl is once more placed
in the water for another shot, and is hauled in about break
of day ; and while it has been at work the previous haul of
fish have been more carefully gone over, and packed in
trunks or boxes, to await the arrival of the steam clipper,
which comes to the fleet to carry the produce to market.
A rather dangerous part of the fishermen's work is the
ferrying of these boxes from the smack to the steamer
in a small boat—too small certainly for such work ; but
as the fish must be got to market, the men must risk their
lives, no matter how wild the water may be during the time
that kind of labour is going on. The placing of the fish on
board the steam carrier involves a great amount of work, as
will be obvious enough when the reader is told that as
many as 2800 trunks of fish will occasionally be brought
to market by one of these steam clippers.

The preceding narrative presents only the merest outline of

the labours undergone by the trawl fishermen during their
spells of work, which vary in length in different districts, the
number of voyages not being the same for every smack, nor
are the rewards of labour always the same As a rule the
captain and perhaps his second hand share in the venture,
and are remunerated according to the catch, but different
smack-owners have different modes of dealing with their
hands In order however to give our readers some idea
of the earnings of those engaged in trawling, we may refer
to the terms of the Messrs Hewitt, who own a large fleet of
smacks The writer obtained much valuable information
about shares and modes of payment at Great Grimsby , but
it will be better to take the latest authoritative information
on the subject, and therefore we shall summarise what was
said about the fishing fleet of Messrs. Hewitt by their
manager, Mr. H. Harvey-George, when he was examined
during October last year (1882), by the Sea Fishing Trade
Committee. As was stated by that gentleman, the men
employed by the Messrs Hewitt (570), are all paid on the
share system, the rates of pay for the different classes being
as follows :—There is first the skipper , his standing wages
and poundage is as follows : if the catch fetches under
100*l.*, 1*s*. in the 1*l* ; if under 150*l.*, 1*s* in the 1*l* on the 100*l.*,
and a fifth on the 50*l.* ; if over 150*l* one-fifth on the total.
The mate gets 14*s* a week and his poundage is : under 100*l*,
5*d* in the 1*l* ; under 150*l.*, 5*d.* on the 100*l* and 7*d.* on the
50*l.* ; if over 150*l*, 7*d.* on the total. The third hand has
14*s*. a week and 4*d.* in the 1*l.* ; and the fourth hand 10*s*. a
week and 3*d.* in the 1*l.* , the fifth hand 9*s* , and 2*d.* in the 1*l.* ;
the sixth hand 8*s* , and 2*d.* in the 1*l.* ; and the cabin boy 7*s*. a
week, and 1*d* in the 1*l.* These per-centages are paid on
the total earnings of the vessel , and the smacks of the firm

are all excellent boats, costing when new from a thousand to twelve hundred pounds, whilst the value of the steam carriers will not be less than £6000 each.

The amount of capital invested by the Messrs Hewitt is about £100,000, and their steam clippers take the fish direct to London. The time of a trawler at the fishing varies from five to eight weeks, during which of course the carrier collects the fish day by day. We have not the means of knowing the earnings of individuals for all the hard and dangerous work they undergo, but we question if, in numerous instances, it will amount to much over a guinea a week— no great sum, when it is taken into account that the men have to sail the ship and work in the rigging as well as attend to the trawl-net, which, as has been indicated, is a most formidable instrument of fish-capture. It can be gathered from the evidence taken by the Sea-Fishing Trade Committee, that many of the Grimsby men feel irritated at not receiving prompt payment of their shares, and, above all, at not being presented with proper details of the sales. In one case, where a man asked to see the settling bill, "the skipper threatened to put him out of the window." As to the food given to the fisher lads aboard the trawling smacks, it is very plain and roughly served, but it is good, and consists of fish in the morning, with biscuits and butter, beef and pies and duff for dinner, and fish again at night. There are other trawling fleets than those of the Messrs. Hewitt engaged in the North Sea—the Hull Steam Fishing Company and Great Northern Steam Fishing Company for instance have 250 smacks at work, the London Fishing Company works 125 vessels and four steam carriers, these in addition to the numerous vessels of the Messrs. Hewitt make up a fishing navy of large figures, and when the single boats fishing on " their own hook," that is boats unconnected with any of the fleets, are added, together with numerous Dutch and other foreign fishing ships, it will be obvious that the German Ocean is a wonderful arena of fishery work.

Having gone over the round of labour incidental to trawling, we shall now proceed on board a cod-man, in order to see how it fares with the line-fishers, who contribute a large proportion of the prime fish which are so much prized for table use.

THE NORTH SEA FISHERS—THE COD-MEN.

Angling on a wholesale scale—A fishing line eight miles long—The value of live Codfish—Small percentage of fish to hooks—Cost of the cod smacks—Remuneration of line fishers—Bait : its importance and scarcity—Mussels and Mussel culture—Fishermen of all work —The shell-fish fisheries, their money value.

ANOTHER branch of industry which yields employment to a large number of fishermen, and incidentally, in Scotland at least, to their wives and families, is line-fishing for cod and other fishes. This is a comparatively simple although probably a very ancient mode of fishing—it is angling on a wholesale scale. On board of the codmen we usually find a larger crew than we do on board of the trawlers, and while out on a voyage, the men, ten or eleven, find plenty of work ; in long line fishing, for instance, it is a serious labour of itself to bait the hooks. A suite of lines is 7200 fathoms in length, or about eight miles long, and it carries the amazing number of 4680 hooks, which have to be carefully baited with whelks, or, as in Scotland, mussels, of which mollusk one Scottish fishing port alone requires over five millions annually. As the hooks are baited, which is a work of time, giving employment to the whole of the crew when not otherwise accomplished, they are very carefully laid aside on trays ready for use, each tray containing so many pieces. A large number of separate lines are used, each being fastened together as a string. At about half-tide the line is shot by being carefully paid overboard so

that none of the snoods to which the hooks are attached
may become fouled. After the hooks have been got into
the water, the smack heaves to till the tide has about
ceased, when the work of hauling in the lines begins, the
vessel making short tacks along the course during the
process, the fish are taken off the hooks as they come in,
this is work that has to be very carefully gone about, as
one living cod is worth a good many dead ones. To keep
these fish alive is therefore the chief aim and end of cod
fishing. As soon as a cod is safely secured, its air blad-
der requires to be punctured in order to admit of its
keeping its equilibrium when, as is immediately done, it is
placed in the well of the vessel in the hope of keeping it
alive till the port is reached, where, along with all the others
which have been captured, it is transferred to a wooden
box or cage in the dock. We are speaking at present of
the cod fishery as prosecuted from Great Grimsby, in one
of the harbours or docks of which thousands of these fish
are kept alive to await the orders of the dealers—they can
be taken out and killed as required   These fish command
an excellent price, and can of course be sold at times when,
in consequence of squally weather preventing fishing, there
might be none to meet the demand   With favourable
weather and an industrious crew good hauls of codfish are
obtained, as well as ling, haddock and halibut. A Great
Grimsby master of a cod smack told the writer that he has
come into port on two or three turns right off the reel with
as many as twenty-two score of live codfish in prime
condition. The skipper alluded to says a very small percentage of fish to the hundred hooks is now taken,
"the dogs" are so voracious that they kill and damage
a lot of the cod, whilst other animals seem to have a
pretty taste for the bait and to be endowed with sufficient

cunning to get it off the hooks without being themselves captured.

The long lines are used in the winter season in various parts of the North Sea, some of them very far apart, whilst there are vessels that venture to great distances in pursuit of codfish, not, however, with any view of bringing the fish home alive, as that would be impossible under the circumstances, and therefore they are salted or cured in some particular way, so that they may be marketable, and bring a profit to those who capture them. The vessels alluded to make a voyage to Iceland or the Faroe Islands, on these occasions the fishing is carried on by means of handlines. At home, what we may call the coast fishing for cod is carried on during the summer months, when the smacks (the same vessels as are used in winter) keep from about ten to twenty five miles off the shore, using the handlines. The number of men employed at this season is the same as in the winter fishery, and it is found that the best fishing is obtained about sunset, at which time all hands will be found industriously at work. We have not entered into any of the technicalities of line fishing, as the business we have now in hand is to give an account of the work achieved by the fishermen and of the remuneration which they receive for performing it. The cod smacks in England—we are speaking of those of Great Grimsby—of which we have personal knowledge, are all of them boats of considerable value, costing, with their appliances, as much probably as £1600, and it is only because of the high money value which codfish commands that men go to such expense to carry on what is at its best a very speculative business and of the small profits of which they complain very much. It is only the captain of a liner who is paid by a share of the profits, his proportion, we were

E

told by one of the Great Grimsby smack-owners, is not quite ten per cent —in fact, his share is an eleventh—of the proceeds of each trip; the hands are all paid fixed wages, the mate twenty-two shillings, and the men each 1*l.* per week. In addition to these wages they are provided with food.

Scottish fishermen industriously pursue the white-fish fishing at all times when cod and other round-fish are in season : in almost every little bay and firth there are boats that fish for the fresh-fish markets, and sell their produce on landing to the buyers for the English salesmen , some of these boats make pretty long voyages, and remain out for two or three days, but the necessity of selling their fish while they are newly caught, urges them to run to port as often as possible. The life led by such fishermen is laborious and hazardous, from the occasional sudden storms which prevail in the northern seas, where they ply their occupation. There are also persons on the coasts of Scotland who fish for cod and ling, but these fishers being far from the market have no alternative but to *cure* their catch, and this is one of the branches of fishing industry which is taken cognisance of by the Scottish Fishery Board, and of which statistics are collected every year.

One of the chief factors in the cod and ling fishery is " bait." Without bait the cod-men are unable to pursue their vocation, and throughout Scotland the gathering of bait used to be an " industry " of great pith and moment, and to-day the delay in procuring bait often keeps the men at home when they would willingly be at sea. In former times the women and children of every fishing community might be seen daily on the coast left bare by the sea, engaged in gathering mussels for the lines ; the Scotch people have long been wedded to the mussel, as they consider it the very best bait for the purposes of fish capture. The labour endured was all the harder, as the women and children often required to trudge a distance of four or five miles, and then having filled their creels with the coveted mollusk they had to walk home again with their heavy loads, after which each family would have to bait perhaps a thousand hooks to be ready against the time of the men's departure to the fishery. Now, when all the accessible mussel supplies have been used up, the men have to procure their bait from private mussel-beds, going as far for it as the Clyde, or the Humber, and, what is of importance to them, they have to pay for what they require, which being taken into account with the time required to make a run to the Humber or the Clyde from the Firth of Forth, considerably diminishes their earnings. It is surprising the fishermen of Scotland do not manage to make a "new departure" in the matter of bait , there are other baits that would attract the fish as much as the mussel, such as a cut of herring or some other fish.* The Dutch, for instance, who are industrious fishers, use the valuable Lampern very largely, for the purpose of baiting their hooks, importing it even from the coast of England, whilst the Americans find excellent bait in the Menhaden. It is surely a curious incident of fishing economy that our men should export bait lamperns to Holland and import mussels from Hamburg! But if the Scottish fishermen who are slow to change will insist upon having mussels at all times for bait, they should

---

* They are now, we are glad to learn, finding out that the White fish when hungry, which is always, are not particular as to their food. The codfish is said to subsist mostly on herrings. Why then do not our fisher folk use the herring more liberally than they do as bait ? It would surely pay them well, on the principle of throwing a sprat to catch a whale to buy two pennyworth of herring to capture two shillings' worth of cod or ling.

project a mussel-farm, and grow these mollusks in quantities, sufficient not only to bait their hooks but to sell to the public as well. In this they can follow the fashion of the French, who have a fine mussel-farm in the Bay of Aiguillon, near La Rochelle, where large quantities of mussels are annually grown on a simple plan, which might very easily be copied by the Scottish fishermen, and so save them a world of labour, anxiety, and expense. In a " Report on the Fisheries of Norfolk," the late Mr. Buckland, in 1875, gave us some particulars of the value of a mussel-bed in the statistics which he published of the Mussel Fisheries of Lynn, these yield from three to four thousand tons in good years, the average price per ton being a pound. There is a very productive natural mussel-bed at Montrose in Scotland which yields a large supply of bait.

The Messrs. Johnston, a local and enterprising firm, the late Mr Buckland told us in one of his reports, have wisely instituted Mussel culture there, and there is a great demand from Peterhead to Fraserburgh for Montrose Mussels, the fishermen of these places taking from 100 to 200 baskets, which they lay down on the rocks as store bait. The mode of measuring these mollusks is by heaping them in a conical form in a herring basket, twenty full baskets making a ton. The fishery officer at Eyemouth (Scotland) reported, in 1879, "the supply of mussels for bait is falling off greatly, and on several occasions lately our fishermen have been laid ashore for want of bait, and the want is becoming greater every day." It will afford an excellent idea of the labour involved in baiting, when it is stated that, in the course of one week, the Eyemouth and Burnmouth boats used for baiting their long lines 61 tons of mussels. That quantity of bait, it may be chronicled here, yielded these fishermen cod and whiting to the value of £2,500, which shows the importance of the bait supply. The labour to all concerned in using such a vast number of mussels must have been enormous.

The collecting of whelks, to serve as bait for the cod-fishers and other uses, is a regular trade on some parts of the English coast, in which a considerable number of small vessels are constantly employed. Each of the cod-smacks takes in a large supply as they start on their fishing tour; during the season of long-line fishing about forty *wash* of these buckies is required; a *wash*, it should be explained, is a measure which contains twenty-one quarts of whelks. These shell-fish are preserved alive in the well of the cod-smack, being kept in bags made of netting till required; they make capital bait, as when once properly affixed on the hooks they are ill to remove. The whelks are caught in various ways, and give employment to a large number of industrious persons, whose business it is to procure them; indeed, so actively is the taking of these animals engaged in, that the supplies of a district soon begin to fall off, so that new fishing grounds have to be sought for every now and then; in the sea lochs of the west of Scotland there are immense numbers of shell-fish, which might either be brought to the food market or be collected for bait.

The foregoing facts and figures, it is hoped by the writer, will enable all who peruse them to form an idea of the incessant work which is involved in the capture of fish. Besides the fishing industries which have been already referred to, as affording fields of labour more or less remunerative to the working fishermen, there are others, such as the mackerel fishery, which might also be placed in evidence, but drifting and seining, no matter what the fish sought for may be, is ever the same, and it would only be treading a beaten path to do more than say that. Happily enough the seasons for fish taking are so varied that industrious fishermen may at all times find abundant work, when wind and water prove suitable.   Thousands of resident fishermen are men of all work taking the different fishes in their seasons, going to sea day by day with an anxious mind, and well pleased many of them are, if they can obtain a moderate catch of fish.   It would surprise those persons unacquainted with the round of fishing labour, to know the extent of the shrimp fishery, and the money value of the shrimps which are caught on our coasts, then there are the annually recurring industries of Oyster dredging, and Lobster and Crab catching, which occupy the time of many persons who prefer that sort of work to the more laborious occupation of herring fishing, or trawling in the prolific North Sea.

THE IRISH FISHER FOLK.

Number of persons engaged in Irish Fisheries—Increase of Irish boats engaged in fishing for Mackerel—Abundance of Pilchards—Cost of carriage of fish—Irish Salmon fisheries—Shell-fish fisheries— The reproductive Loan Fund—Its success—Social habits of the Irish Fisher Folk—The Claddagh

THE number of persons employed in the Irish fisheries in the year 1846 was 113,073, who were in possession of a fleet of 19,883 boats and vessels of various kinds. These were the persons supposed to be actively engaged in prosecuting the various fisheries of Ireland ; were we to take into account their families and dependents we would be able, we daresay, to make up the total number to a figure beyond half a million.

The number of persons fishing and the number of boats have greatly decreased since 1846. According to the last published report of the Inspectors of Irish fisheries, it appears that during 1882, the number of registered vessels in Ireland fishing for sale was 6089, with crews numbering 21,597 men, and 794 boys. Of these 1978 vessels, 7310 men and 401 boys are returned as having been exclusively employed in fishing, and 4111 vessels, 14,287 men, and 393 boys as partially engaged.

These figures must not be accepted for more than they are worth ; the Inspectors do all they can to ensure their being correct, but various difficulties lie in the way of obtaining accurate statistics. They explain in one of their reports that great irregularities had occurred in carrying out the registration of boats and vessels since 1842, so much so indeed as to render the returns of no practical value "It was the practice some years ago," says the Inspectors in their report for 1876, "to register and return, as boats and vessels engaged in the fisheries, every boat in the different divisions, whether used for cutting seaweed, carrying passengers, turf, sand, or other commodities, fishing or pleasure, and a crew was assigned to each without ascertaining if such actually existed, no proper comparison can therefore be made between the numbers actually engaged in sea fishing during the past and former years." Since 1846 the number of boats, and, of course, the number of persons employed in their management as well, have steadily declined ; in 1856 the fleet of boats numbered 11,069, manned by 48,774 men and boys ; in 1866 the numbers respectively were 9444 (boats) and 40,663 (crews). By the year 1876 the reduction was still more marked, the numbers being as follows : Craft of all descriptions engaged in fishing for sale 5965, with crews numbering 22,773 men, and 920 boys.

In looking into the details of Irish fishing as conducted to-day, we find some reliable statistics of the number of boats taking part in the herring and mackerel fisheries, the latter in particular being a growing industry in the Irish seas, the importance of which has been largely divined by the local fishermen. At the various herring fishing stations, we find a total of 734 Irish boats engaged between May and December, the number of the crew in each boat not being given, but there would probably not be less than 4000 in all, men and boys together. The number of Irish vessels taking part in the capture of mackerel in 1882 was 263 ; as against 327 English and Manx and 25 Scottish boats. In 1876, the number of Irish boats fishing for mackerel was only 133, showing an increase in the fleet in seven years equal to about a hundred per cent, which is very gratifying, and proves that the Irish fishermen are prompt to seize upon an obvious advantage. The mackerel fishery gives employment to many other persons besides those who capture the fish. At the chief ports, Kinsale and Baltimore, vessels are employed in bringing ice : then there are the carrying steamers, each with a fair crew on board, whilst considerable employment is given to residents in the respective localities both in packing the fish and in other ways.

It is expected that the Irish fishermen will in time grow a pilchard fishery. Large shoals of these fish are known to be in the Irish seas, and a beginning of fishery enterprise in that line has already taken place, fifty-four hogsheads of Pilchards having been cured in the Cornish fashion (1882), at Baltimore, which were sold in Genoa, and realised at the rate of £4 14s. per hogshead. As the inspectors of the Irish fisheries say, there is abundance of room for this enterprise being largely developed off the county of Cork, and the foregoing should be an encouragement to others to embark in it ; if judiciously managed by persons who understand the best methods of capturing and curing, it ought to prove most remunerative.

No statistics of a reliable kind are published as to the number of boats and men engaged in the round and flat fish fisheries of Ireland, but testimony has been frequently borne as to the abundance of many kinds of valuable food fishes in the waters surrounding the Emerald Isle, and of the field of industry thus presented to the Irish fisher folk. But although the finest turbot and holibut are to be had for the mere exertion of capture, the Irish fisher folk are not possessed, in most instances, of the necessary fishing

gear with which to catch them ; at some places the boats
and machinery of capture are of the most fragile description,
and if improved vessels were to be provided there are no
fitting harbours in which they could be received, whilst the
distance of many of the seats of fishing from a profitable
market is another serious drawback to the advancement of
fishing enterprise in Ireland.   Thus the fisher folks of Ireland
are heavily handicapped in every way they desire to turn
themselves.   As an instance of how the men are held down
we may state, on the authority of the inspectors, that in June
1881, two consignments, consisting of 19 and 30 boxes of
mackerel respectively, each containing 120 fish, were sent
up from the county of Cork to Dublin at a charge of 5*l.* 2*s.*
1*d.* and 7*l.* 14*s.* respectively, and the balances remitted to
the senders were 11*s.* 11*d.* in one case and 1*l.* 6*s.* in the
other, making a total of 1*l* 17*s.* 11*d.* for 5,880 fish, or about
three of these fine fish for a farthing.   The value of the
cod fish caught by the Irish fishermen, and exported to
England during the year 1882, amounted, in round figures,
to 389,240*l.* 10*s.*

The Irish Salmon Fisheries afford employment to many
persons, the total yield of these fine fish being considerable,
far in advance even of Scotland.   The estimated money
value of the salmon captured in Irish waters has been set
down of late years (1882 excepted) as being considerably
above half a million sterling, a fact which, we think, is not
generally known.   There is one branch of fishing which
might, we think, afford remunerative employment to a
large number of persons, namely, that for crabs, which
might be carried on in such a way as to be independent
of early markets, as these crustaceans might be stored in
rudely constructed ponds to be kept till called for.   Could
the crabs of Ireland be brought to English ports they

would undoubtedly command a ready sale at remunerative rates. Lobsters, too, abound amid the rocks of the Irish seas, they are well known to commerce, but still larger quantities of these delicious crustaceans might we think be brought to market; traps for their capture are easy to construct, and any kind of garbage will do for bait.

An interesting feature of fishery economy in Ireland is centred in what is called the "Irish reproductive loan fund," by which sums of money are advanced to the fishermen to be repaid at a given time, the amounts received being again advanced to other fishermen. Much good has been by this means achieved. We have not space in which to trace the history of the fund, or to describe the machinery of distribution, but we may, abridging the information given by the inspectors in some of their annual reports, state that in particular instances the poor fishermen who have been obliged with loans have been able to turn the money to excellent account in providing the necessary fishing gear of which they were utterly deficient. "In vast numbers of cases," says Mr. Inspector Brady, "but for the loans, I believe the people on the west coast would have been obliged to abandon fishing altogether, and if so had no other resources." The Irish fisher folk have also had the advantage of obtaining substantial assistance from another fund, namely, the money voted by the Dominion of Canada for the relief of distress in Ireland. This fund amounted to £20,500 and was placed in the hands of a Committee who devoted nearly £10,000 to the promotion of piers and the improvement of harbours, and £11,000 to the purchase of fishing gear and new boats and the repairing of old ones. This loan has been the means of effecting a great amount of good: in one locality, to which £200 worth of nets were sent and distributed among fifty men, over £1,200 worth of Mackerel were taken in one month. In another locality a very poor man to whom a boat and net were given, costing only £12, realised in three nights by herring fishing, nearly £60. The inspector, after great experience of their working, says, "every year's experience still further convinces me of the great importance of these loans to poor fishermen. In my opinion their fishing pursuits are far more valuable than their farming, and both can be carried on together with great advantage, not only to the people themselves who follow this pursuit as a part of their means of living, but to the country at large by the production of a large quantity of valuable food." It is to be hoped, from what is known of the really beneficial results flowing from such aid, that still more will be forthcoming ; there is undoubtedly a great field of enterprise open to the Irish fisher-folk, even taking into account the poor harbour accommodation, and the distances at which pro-fitable markets have to be sought.

The Irish fisher folk, as a class, are singularly honest and virtuous, not so much given to dissipation or riotous behaviour as has been asserted, and whenever a prospect of fair reward is held out for labour expended, they will embark in any fishing enterprise. As was recently said of the Irish fisherman, the man who voluntarily seeks his living on the sea, cannot be wanting in aptitude for work, courage, or perseverance against adverse circumstances. The Irish fisher folk are much the same to-day in their social habits as they were centuries ago. Their sanitary surround-ings are not of the best, and their superstitions and prejudices are much the same, more intensified, perhaps, if that be possible, than those of their Scottish and Cornish brethren. A well-known member of the Society of Friends (Mr. Allen, Black Rock, near Dublin) it is interesting to know, has borne important testimony to the good behaviour of the Irish fisher folk ; being asked if he had ever known any cases of Irish fishermen being implicated in Agrarian outrages, his answer was to the effect that during a period of fifty years he had not known a solitary case of an Irish fisherman being charged as an accomplice in any of these crimes.

At the Claddagh—in a portion of Galway situated on the right of the harbour, we find all that pertains to the social habits of the Irish fisher folk brought to a focus , the colony of fishermen which is there established still retain among them the customs of their remote ancestors. The town is a peculiar looking place, an extraordinary collection of cottages thatched with straw, and the people who inhabit these abodes are totally distinct in dress, habits, and customs, from those of the town (Galway). The peculiar dress of the women imparts a singularly foreign aspect to the streets and quays, and the person elected by the fisher people as their Mayor, is implicitly obeyed, he is of course one of themselves, and is able to regulate the community, and settle disputes according to their own peculiar laws and customs. On occasions of difference, his decision is so much valued, that law is seldom resorted to. Like the fisher folk of the Scottish and Northumbrian coasts, the people of Claddagh are great believers in luck, and in signs and omens, and in all matters of dispute, they stand firmly by each other, even when one of them is wrong. Strangers are not made welcome as residents in the fisher quarter of Galway, in fact, they are not allowed to reside within the bounds of the Claddagh. The people inter-marry, and no marriage, we believe, is considered to be properly brought about unless preceded by an elopement ; the bride is presented by way of dowry, with a boat or share of a boat, according to the means of her parents, and the wedding ring is an heir-loom of the family ; it is transferred from mother to daughter, the first married, and so on to their descendants.   The Claddagh people, after the fashion of their foreign brethren, hold occasional fêtes and make merry on the occasion of electing their Mayor or King and sheriffs.   The Mayor is completely one of themselves, but when at sea he acts as admiral, and, as we have said, his word in most things is law.   When out fishing, the Claddagh men carry in their boats no strong drink of any kind—no spirits or malt liquors.

With these few details of this curious place, we take our leave of the Irish fisher folk, heartily wishing them a great increase of prosperity.

THE FOREIGN FISHER FOLK.

Peculiarities of the Foreign Fisher-folk — Roman and Athenian Fishwives—Fêtes of the Foreign Fisher people—Italian Fishers— French Fisher-folk—Madame Picard the poetical fish-wife—The Dutch Fishwives—The Norwegian Fishers—Chinese fishery arrangements.

HAVING sketched at considerable length the round of labour from day to day of our own fishermen, we may now refer to the foreign fisher folk, who are quite as peculiar in their habits and modes of life as the persons we have just been describing—they are people, in fact, no matter in what country we find them, who live for themselves among themselves, steadily transmitting from one generation to another their stereotyped manners and customs ; their vices and their virtues, their belief in signs and omens, and the varied traditions of their ancient calling. From the earliest days of Greek and Roman civilisation, those who gather the harvest of the sea have formed in every country where they dwell a caste by themselves, and to-day they are much the same as we read of their being centuries ago—for fishing is a vocation of the remotest antiquity.

In all matters pertaining to their modes of life and commercial dealings the ancient fishwives were very much alike —no matter to what country they belonged the family likeness was marked and unmistakable. Thus the Roman fishwives were a counterpart of those of ancient Athens, and those of the " Modern Athens " of to-day may be taken

as tolerably exact copies, if not in costume, at least in
manners, customs and language, of their classic prototypes.
Juvenal of course satirises the fish dealers of ancient Rome,
taking for illustration a tender point of their character—
namely the freshness of their wares. He depicts a dealer in
fish as praying that he may be fed —

> " On the loved features of his infant's head
> Soused in Egyptian vinegar, if aught
> Against his fishes' freshness can be brought."

A fondness for fêtes and demonstrations has ever been a
marked characteristic of foreign fishers. When Pope Leo
the Tenth was summoned to the Papal throne in 1513 the
Roman fisherwives held a fête ; going in a body in order
to offer his Holiness their congratulations, and flatter him
by a declaration of their loyalty. In a graceful speech the
Pope returned his best compliments and thanks, telling
them that, as the successor of an ancient fisherman of the
sea of Galilee, he took a particular interest in their calling,
which, had for its object the providing of many chief
necessaries of daily life as well as a large portion of the
luxuries of the table. The Venetian fishwives used also
to hold grand Carnival every year during the season of
Lent. Their merrymaking lasted for three days, and, whilst
it continued the women dressed themselves in their richest
apparel, displaying at the same time as great an array of
costly jewellery as they possibly could The Venetian fishwives were likewise noted for their uncivil tongues and
their tendency to get into " rows " of all kinds, as well as
for their constant and exceedingly voluble vituperation of
the authorities.

Scattered allusions to the Italian fisheries may be found
occasionally in the pages of the classic writers of the fif-
teenth century ; they are all of the same tenor, and harp on

the bad manners and worse morals of the fishwives of the period, dwelling more especially on their unruly habits and powers of extortion Another fisher-fête of the olden time (and one indeed which is worthy of mention, and is still perpetuated with many of the old ceremonies) was that held by the men and women who dwelt amid the great series of lagoons at Commachio at the mouth of the river Po, just where that river falls into the Adriatic. The great eel farm of Commachio is one of those " specialties " of fishing industry which were common a few centuries ago It is still in existence, and the manners and customs of its inhabitants are said to be almost unchanged, being nearly the same to-day as they were four or five centuries ago. On the day following the nights during which they obtain a great catch of their particular fish—the eel—the population of the lagoon usually hold high festival, and indulge in a fête, with church-going processions and other rejoicings The fisher people of Commachio are much like those of other fishing communities, " they have," to quote a graphic but vulgar phrase, " a spice of the devil in their constitution."

The fisher folk of the Italian coast are still very much like what they were five or six centuries ago ; they deal, as a matter of course, in the same goods as their ancestors dealt in, their business being of an hereditary nature ; and to-day they trade in exactly the same fashion as their forefathers traded five hundred years ago One has only to visit the fish-markets of the coast towns to be convinced of the fact. The fishermen of the period pat the tunny in the same way as their predecessors did. They do this while the fish is in the net, just in the same way as one would pat a favourite dog or horse ; they say it makes the giant fish more docile than it would otherwise be. It is said that the

F

old fishermen used to ride on the back of the fish within the circumference of the net !

The scenes to be witnessed in many of the Italian fish-markets are exceedingly grotesque, and the noise of quarrelling and the general loquacity that seems to be incident to the sale of the *frutti della mare* in the fish-market of Venice in the nineteenth century is of the very choicest order of "Billingsgate," and certainly cannot even be surpassed by the notorious fish-hawkers of Dublin of whom Dean Swift wrote—

> " All mad to speak, with none to hearken—
> They set the very dogs a-barking ;
> No chattering makes so loud a din
> As fishwives o'er a cup of gin."

A large portion of the Italian population earn a livelihood by fishing, some of the men using the frailest of boats, craft which can only be used in the finest of weather. The number of men engaged in sea fisheries on December 31, 1869, with the exclusion of the then Papal States, was 60,000, employing 18,000 boats, and giving a mean annual produce of forty million lire. In addition to the sea fisheries, there are lagoon and estuary fishing industries, which employ many persons ; whilst some of the fishing products, as the Sponge, Pinna and Coral, bear of course no relation to the food supplies. As a matter of act Italy imports fish from Great Britain and other countries, to the extent of more than twenty-one million lire

Taking leave of Italy, we come to France, where a few hundred years ago many different laws were enacted for the regulation of *les poissardes ;* and they undoubtedly required to be legislated for, as they too were in the habit of exercising the same vehemence of rhetoric which is the common inheritance of the piscatorial sisterhood. The *poissonières* of Paris have often figured in the history of that turbulent city. Certain parts of Lutetia had, in the olden time, a most pronounced " fish-like smell," and remains have at various times been found which indicate the antiquity of the fishmongers' craft in the capital of France. At a very early period the fishwives of Paris were divided into two classes, the one being called *harengères* or sellers of salted herrings, the other class, known as *poissonières*, being dealers in various kinds of fresh fish. The two classes, as may be readily supposed, were always quarrelling ; and at times, their rancour was so fierce that their quarrels often ended in bloodshed and murder. Some curious laws were enacted by St. Louis for regulating the sales of fish. First of all, the right to sell had to be purchased from or be granted by the king. Wise men (*prudhommes*) were appointed by his Majesty's *chef de cuisine* to look after the fish dealers, and to amerce in a fine such as sold without permission of the king. The grand cook of his Majesty likewise forced all the *prudhommes* who were chosen, to take an oath that they would see to the price of the fish supplied to the royal tables, being fixed upon " soul and conscience." The French fish-dealers of those days were so far happy, inasmuch as they were officially blessed by the Cardinal of Paris, his bishops and clergy, once every year ; the occasion of course being chosen for the celebration of a grand fête by the fish-sellers, the boatmen of the river, the fisher-folks of Havre, and those of other ports near the mouth of the Seine. Such ceremonies are still, we believe, observed at Marseilles and other portions of the continental seaboard. Similar fêtes and processions used long ago to be of frequent occurrence in various Scottish fishing towns, but although the fisher people of some particular fishing ports may march once a year in a procession, the custom of general holidays is falling into abeyance.

It is interesting to learn that one hundred and seventy three years since there was a commanding fish-selling population in the French capital. Of oyster-women there were at that time no less than four thousand, and if so the sale of the toothsome bivalve must have been so enormous as to warrant speculation as to where they all came from. It is not surprising with such a *corps* of vendors that the natural oyster scalps of the French coast came in time to be exhausted! It is almost superfluous to say that the Parisian fisher-wives, like their sisters all over the world, " enjoyed " a rather bad character, and were stigmatised as adepts at cheating their customers. They could, by the exercise of a little *finesse*, deprive the ready-eating buyer of two or three of the best oysters out of every dozen he might purchase, by pretending they were bad, and kindly eating them for him. They used also to introduce into their commercial system a few empty shells, the oysters of which had just been sold to another customer, and, counting them, pretend their patron had eaten the full tale of his bargain. It would be unjust to omit mention in this chronicle of Madame Picard, a Parisian fishwife, famed for her wit and poetic talents, who flourished in the middle of the last century, and who, being frequently in their society, was personally known to Voltaire and other great authors of the day. Her poetry, if we may believe the critics of the period, was not devoid of genius; it was chiefly of an amatory and sentimental description. Her poetical works were published in the year 1768. Madame ultimately left her fish-stall to become the wife of a silk and lace merchant, in which position she was much respected.

There is to-day a large fishing population in France, all

of whom as a rule are good at their business, and many of
them fish so near us that we are able to judge. The fisher-
folk of France are much like their brethren of Scotland
and Northumberland, superstitious and peculiar. The
French have an extensive fishing fleet, over twenty-two
thousand vessels, which require more than 80,000 fishermen
to work them. As in Scotland, the French fishers are
always aided in their business by their women folk, and in
all fishing communities on the French coasts, the round of
fisher life and labour is much the same as we know it at
home, there are times of consuming anxiety for the women,
when the men are at sea, and have been delayed in bringing
home their catch by a sudden storm. The short and simple
annals of fisher life in France, and other foreign lands, are
as much tinged with melancholy, as the lives of the toilers of
the sea on the coasts of Great Britain and Ireland. Each
little village has experienced its terrible tragedies arising
out of the fateful work of those who draw their daily bread
from out the waters.

Holland, the cradle of fishery enterprize, can of course
boast of its fishwives , the fishing villages on the sea board
of the German Ocean, as well as those on the coast of the
Zuyder Zee, are well worth a visit from the curious. The
fisher quarter of Schevening is exceedingly quaint and
peculiar, and the fishwives of Holland, and Belgium as
well, are just as peculiar as those of the French or Scottish
coasts, having their own specialties of living, and being
largely imbued with the familiar superstitions of their
craft. We cannot say if a Dutch fishwife can find
" tongues in trees" or " books in the running brooks," but
we do know that she can read the clouds and interpret the
mists that veil the heavens : and the wailing of the water-
fowl or the plaintive cry of the curlew will raise a vein of

superstition that cannot be allayed except by cessation from work. The Dutch fisherman has ever the recollection of a crowd of death-dealing disasters upon his memory as he lazily whistles for a wind or murmurs a prayer to hush the rising breeze. The fisherwives of Holland are exceedingly industrious: they carry the fish caught by their husbands, brothers or sons to market, and negotiate the sales. The work of the husband is finished as soon as he comes on shore, the work of the women then commences. The wives undergo great labour, and take much pains to render it remunerative; but the fisherwomen of South Holland do not look so happy or prosperous as their sisters located on the shores of the Zuyder Zee, who, as a rule, are in a far more flourishing condition. At Moniekendam, and on the opposite island of Marken, the fisher people afford ample scope for study and portraiture. They are quaint in their dress, peculiar in their manners, and exceedingly simple and pious. The men of Marken are very temperate, are the finest sailors in the world, and live to a good age. The colony of fisher folk established there is similar to some of those in Scotland: it is a kind of family community, like that of Newhaven near Edinburgh. The people intermarry each with the other, and thus beget habits as stereotyped in many respects as those of the Chinese, or the nest-building birds of the air. Their wants being few and simple, and the temptations to expend money rare, the people of the very remarkable island of Marken happily find themselves passing rich.

The Dutch fishers are always at work when wind and tide are suitable, and that they fish for other markets than their own is well-known; they send us a liberal share of their catch in the shape of Turbot, Eels, &c. Even so far back as half a century ago, we paid them nearly £100,000 per

annum for the " Aldermanic fish," and the lobsters of which
the sauce was made. The Dutch cure their herrings on
board of their fishing luggers, which industry keeps the
fishermen very busy, the Dutch cured herring are very fine,
they are pickled with the crown, gut left in them, and are
much relished. The "busses" remain at the fishing all
the season, the fish being collected from the fleet by small
steamers or "Yagers" as they are called, which bear them
rapidly to port, and the herrings which first come to hand
of the year's fishing, are highly esteemed and command a
high price, a barrel specially prepared being sent for the use
of the royal family. In former times a substantial reward
was always bestowed on the fishers who were earliest in the
market with their herrings.

We have not space in which to describe even in the briefest
possible manner all the foreign fisheries, but by way of
giving variety to these memoranda, we may here indicate
the labour which is incidental to one phase of the cod
fishery of the Lofoten Islands, namely, "the gill net fishery,"
and we hope that mode of taking cod-fish will be introduced
by our own fishermen who are so often put to straits for that
expensive property of their work—*bait.* Gill-net fishing for
cod is a Norwegian industry of considerable antiquity, it is
reputed, at any rate, to have been introduced as far back as
1485, and is now practised extensively along the coasts of
Norway, but especially at the islands we have named, where
cod at certain seasons resort, it is said, in literal millions, the
inward "rush" of the fish being hailed by those interested
with great delight ; it is almost needless to say that the time
of capture is the spawning season of the fish. Gill-net fishing is carried on from open boats, each with a crew of six or
eight men, and carrying from sixty to a hundred nets, which,
however, are not all used at once, the greater part of them

being held in reserve to fill up the place of those which are lost from accident, or which are being dried after use. About twenty-five of the nets, however, are fastened together, to be set by each boat. These are joined by being riveted at top and bottom, and are kept taut in the water by means of iron sinkers, and floats made of hollow glass, and are so arranged as to be either close to the bottom, or a few feet from it. The men at a signal all start in the afternoon to set their nets in the way described, placing them across the current, the fishermen usually returning to the shore after that work has been satisfactorily accomplished. Then after a few hours' rest, and in the darkness of a night that may be both stormy and bitterly cold, the men start again for the fishing ground, to gather in the fish that may have been caught. This is both exciting and hard work, but it is work which must be accomplished, no matter how the winds may roar, or the waves may leap. The heavily weighted nets are ill to haul on board, especially when well laden with fish, which happily they sometimes are. The catch, however, is exceedingly variable, ranging from a few dozens in a day to a few hundreds for each boat—five hundred fish is thought a good take, and the fish captured in this manner are the very primest of the prime, 200 of which will be equal to 350 of cod taken by the hooks, whilst the livers of the gill-captured fish yield more liberally of oil than those which are taken by means of the trawl.

These fishermen earn more money at the Lofoten cod-fishery than their brethren who handle the lines, or manipulate the trawl, and in consequence there is a growing desire to prosecute that branch of cod fishing It is stated that in 1879 there were 2532 boats engaged in that style of fishing, with crews numbering in all 14,322 men ; in the preceding year the total catch of cod at the Lofoten fishery numbered 24,660,000 fish, and of that quantity upwards of 14,000,000 were taken in the nets   The Norwegians are mighty fishers, industrious and careful, possessing all the virtues of their fellows in other countries ; the fisher folk of Norway number eleven per cent. of the population, about 80,000 persons being employed in getting in the harvest of the sea.

Much curious information about the social condition of the Chinese fishermen, and the economy of the fisheries, so far as the use of gear is concerned is contained in "the Yellow Book," or catalogue of the Chinese collection in the Fishery Exhibition.   We shall not, however, spoil the interest of what is told by any attempt at abridgment—it would require indeed a book as large as this to contain all that might be said descriptive of the Chinese and Oriental fisheries, such as the pearl-diving industry of Ceylon, and the sponge and coral fisheries of tropical seas.

SUMMARY. CONCLUSION.

FROM the details which have been given in the preceding pages, the reader will have learned that no fisherman is able to rule his ways of life, or govern his daily work after the fashions of our land industries. Those who work in factories, members of the building trades, and persons who follow similar occupations, can regulate their hours of labour, so as to begin and leave off work at fixed periods, and to eat their food at fixed hours. Not so the poor fisherman, who is a slave to the winds and the waves: he must wait till the passing storm has exhausted its fury, and the waters have become comparatively calm, before he dare venture in his boat from the harbour, in order to enrich the national commissariat with the "bounty of the waters," and earn the daily bread required by his wife and little ones. And even when he reaches the seat of his labour he may in vain cast his lines into the water. He cannot compel the fish to swallow his lure, they may not indeed be in that part of the waters into which for the time he has dipped his nets, so the disappointed fishers frequently return from a toilsome journey no richer than when they spread their sail to the favouring winds two or three days previously. It is curious that men who have been all their lives at the business will time and again fail to hit upon the fish. There are no certain rules, however, by which they can be found, and he would be a shrewd fisherman who always obtained miraculous draughts. As we have shown, herring fishing is very much of a lottery; of two boats which may side by side be plying their trade, one may find a hundred barrels of fish in its train of netting, while the other may not capture a hundred herrings! So in line fishing and in trawling, the fortunes of the catch are upon occasions singularly varied, huge piles of the fruit of the sea may fall into the nets of Tom, whilst Dick may also obtain a share of the finny spoil, but poor Harry in vain woos fortune on the deep—never a fish—round or flat, comes near his machinery of capture, no gigantic member of the Gadidæ family, no aldermanic turbot rewards his zealous labours.

"Why," it is being asked in various quarters, "should we accord our sympathies to fishermen in a greater degree than to other men, who gain their bread by the sweat of their brow ?" That is a question which it is not, we think, difficult to answer. Fishing is an industry by itself, and those who woo fortune on the waters but seldom find it; fishing being a perilous occupation, which yields but an unsteady reward. It has been said by economists of the Gradgrind school, that "no man is compelled to fish," which is a truism, but if the advice implied in the sneer were to be taken, it would bode no good to the country Happily, it is advice that never will be taken, there have been fishers on the sea since the miraculous draughts were taken from the waters of Galilee, and there will be fishers probably for centuries to come, fishing, we hope, under improved conditions. At the present time the fishing population is still largely leavened by men who are descendants of hereditary fishermen, and who, as well as their fathers before them, have known no other occupation—it is an occupation with which their lives have been mingled, and which they could not change if they were willing. A frequent charge made against fishermen is that they are lazy and extravagant, living when they have the chance a riotous life. The charge is a strained one. As has been indicated, they cannot regulate their hours of work by the sounding of a factory bell, they can only go to sea when the condition of the water is favourable, and when men have had a continuous spell of work, lasting from sixteen to sixty or seventy hours, they require corresponding rest. No fisherman has the privilege of an eight hours' day, like the well-timed mechanic or factory worker ; nor has any fisherman a share of those amenities which fall to the working-class population of towns ; no institutes or cheerful clubs ; no well-filled libraries. The dwelling places of many of the fisher people are often remote from the haunts of civilisation, in hamlets that are utterly destitute of any means of spreading knowledge, and when the fishermen congregate at the larger fishing-ports their work is a work of emergency, which has to be prosecuted with great rapidity, and admits of no time of recreation.

The heroism of such a life as is led by our fishermen from day to day all the year round has never, we think, been so much appreciated as it should be. The dangers of the deep are proverbial, and of these, the toilers of the sea, who bring to land such a magnificent contribution to the national commissariat have a full share, the danger being not a little aggravated by the want of good harbours. The value of the food which is annually brought to us from the waters has been estimated at various large sums— ranging from five to fourteen millions sterling, and taking even the smaller figure, it betokens an amount of enterprise and work which is not a little remarkable—it is so much

wealth to the nation got at first hand—for which we are indebted to the fishermen. At the very least there are on
the coasts of the United Kingdoms half a million persons
dependent on the fisheries for the necessaries of life which
they obtain, and it is their hard fate that only by unceasing
work can the fishers keep up their homes, and feed and clothe
their children, who, along with their mothers, are called upon
to share the daily round of labour, to take part in the toilsome work of net shooting and hauling, or of baiting the
hooks, and who in the end, by means of this combined industry, often do not earn the wages of a single well-employed
mechanic, who pursues his vocation on the dry land, in a
comfortable workshop, with abundance of light and heat
at his own command.

It is not every labouring man who could be a fisherman even if he were to try, fishing is a business which
requires experience, and can only be acquired by training,
so that our best men in this department of industry are
those who are hereditary fishermen. These only have in
the largest measure the properties of endurance and skill
which must ever be incidental to their peculiar occupation.
The fisherman must not only have physical strength, he
must have moral courage as well, for at every hour of the
day he knows he is fighting for his life. Whilst his hand
must be occupied on sail or line, his mind, too, must be
actively at work gathering those scraps of knowledge which
are constantly required for the prosecution of his business,
and by means of which he is endowed with that cunning
and skill which he finds so necessary.

It is not alone the contribution made by our fishermen
to the national commissariat, that falls to be considered in
connection with our fishing fleet. Other benefits accrue to
the nation which cannot be ignored in a work like this,

sketchy and unfilled up, as it may appear ; the building of new boats, and the repair of those now in use, the weaving of nets and the manufacture of sails afford remunerative labour to hundreds of persons. The bringing of salt and barrel-wood to the curing stations, and the exporting of the fish to foreign places, also affords employment to those engaged in that line of business   Nor is the money earned by our fisherman hid away in a napkin ; it is at once put in circulation, and all manner of tradespeople feel the benefit thereof, the owners of their cottages and houses,—many of these, and we regret to have to state the fact, being in a most unsanitary condition—derive their rent, whilst the baker, the butcher, and the clothier, find their tills swelled by the money of the fisher-folks.   Theie are few, indeed, who do not directly, or indirectly, derive some benefit from the " Harvest of the Sea."

In penning these remarks we have no idea of going against the usual dictates of political economy.   We know that men are not " forced to fish " against their wills.   But, as has been shown, many of these men know no better, having been born to the business—never in fact having had an opportunity of trying their fortunes at another trade. It has been asserted by public writers and economists that, fish being so dear, fishermen must earn a great deal of money ; but that reasoning does not avail with those who are behind the scenes.   It is too often but a very scanty share of the price which the public pay for the produce of the sea that actually falls to the share of the fishermen, who incur all the dangers incidental to its capture.   Still the public are the gainers ; they deiive a large amount of wholesome food from the unfathomed caves of ocean, the sale of which helps in some degree to keep down the price of butchers' meat.   And to some extent the fishing interest is of use to the State, as it provides a hardy population of sailors from which the mercantile navy is occasionally récruited, and from which our ships of war, were they not nowadays chiefly manned by mechanics, in the persons of their engineers and stokers, might obtain a supply of sailors. It may be said of our fishing craft generally that they afford a fine training in habits of industry and discipline to thousands of persons who in after years season the population with that independence of character and that love of personal liberty which is so desirable for a free people; and it is a pitiful circumstance that in so many instances a lifetime of arduous labour should only end in abject poverty; it is sad to find, as not infrequently happens, that many a man, whose everyday heroisms would in some other calling have made him famous, has landed in the days of his old age in the workhouse.

We cannot prophesy with any certainty as to the future of our fisheries, but it may be predicted that steam-fishing craft of all kinds will come more into use than has hitherto been the case; and if that should happen, it will in some degree better the position of the fishermen. With steam power they will be able to accomplish their work with a greater degree of speed, and will also be better able to battle against the elements with which they have to contend. Occasional dread catastrophes occur every now and then to our fishing fleets; they are of kin, in their suddenness and terrible fatalities, to the explosions which take place in our coal mines; and at such periods the aid of the charitable is demanded for widows and orphans. It is not our purpose to say one word that would freeze the fountains of benevolence, but is it not time that the fisher folk should accumulate a fund, to be in readiness for such times of need? In some fishing communities there are, we know, "friendly

societies" that offer aid to the distressed, that give a sum for
funeral expenses and an allowance in periods of sickness; a
small payment implies the right to such help as has been arranged for. But, grateful as such aid may be in a time of need,
it is not enough ; and for such a body of men as the British
fishermen to be appealing on every occasion of calamity for
eleemosynary aid is anything but seemly. If they could
but learn to appreciate the power of the pence, they would
find that, with a small weekly contribution from the
hundred thousand persons who are regular fishers such a
sum would in the course of three or four years be accumulated as would set up anew their wrecked boats, provide
for the widow, and educate the fatherless. We would
say to the fisher folk, Do this yourselves ; have your own
accumulated funds managed by your own people. One
penny per week from each one of a hundred thousand
persons would produce, roughly speaking, a sum of over
twenty-one thousand pounds per annum which would be
more than ample for all that will ever be required of it.

It is not the business of the writer to do more than
indicate that such a scheme is quite practicable; the
details may be worked out at leisure, but the sooner the
better. It might even be taken in hand in conjunction,
perhaps, with the issuing of a licence to all fishermen, by some
of our government departments. We have a government
which sends our telegrams, forwards our letters, carries our
parcels, takes care of our savings, and sells us annuities ;
why should it not arrange to assure the lives of our fishermen and to replace their boats when they are destroyed
by the storm? A small sum charged annually for a
"licence to fish" would provide all the funds which are
necessary. Five shillings a year from forty thousand fishermen would amount to ten thousand pounds per annum—

all that might be necessary. With such a sum and its accu-
mulations to fall back upon, fishermen would be independent of the bestowal of public charity. We know that
associations of different kinds have of late years been or-
ganized for the insurance of fishing gear, chiefly the boats,
and smack owners have joined their forces in this direction.
We should be glad to see the fishermen acting in combina-
tion to obtain both a provision for accidents of all kinds,
but for the time of old age as well.

We offered recently in the pages of a popular peri-
odical, the following suggestion for the benefit of the
Scottish fishermen. "There is another way of solving
the question of how the fisher-folk might provide for a
rainy-day. Taking the herring-fishery as the typical fishery
of Scotland, an industry at which, during some portion of
the year, every unit of the fishery population assists, we
may state that the value to the fishermen of the herrings
which they capture can scarcely be less than two millions
of pounds sterling per annum. A million barrels at least
are cured, and large quantities of herring are caught in addition, and sold fresh Accepting the value of the fish to
their captors as being two millions sterling—a barrel, it may
be stated, contains about seven hundred and fifty fish, and
these, at the price of a half-penny each, come to a sum of
thirty-one shillings and threepence ; so that the figure we
have given is by no means an exaggeration—is it too much
to ask of the fishermen that they should devote a sixpence
of the price obtained for each barrel to insurance of boats
and lives ? How much do a million sixpences come to ?
A million sixpences amount to the very handsome total of
twenty-five thousand pounds ; a far larger sum than would,
one year with another, be required ; so that to all appearance, an assessment of threepence, or at the most fourpence,

G

per barrel on the cured fish alone would yield all that is necessary to replace boats and fishing-gear in times of adversity. The Scottish Fishery board—the usefulness of which is sometimes called in question both in parliament and elsewhere—might be intrusted with the collection of the money. The Board has already in active work an organisation for collecting the fees on every barrel of herrings that is branded ; it would not be difficult, therefore, for the officers of the Board to collect whatever sum may be agreed upon from the fishermen."*

In making such suggestions we will probably be met by the answer, that fishery boards, with whom would rest the business of collection, have not the power to interfere in these matters, but the power, we fancy, will not be ill to procure. In Ireland, as has been shown, the fishery inspectors carry on similar work, they administer a fishermen's loan fund, which has been productive of good by enabling persons to obtain boats and fishing gear who could not otherwise have obtained it. There are other means by which fishermen may provide a fund for the proverbial rainy day ; other devices might easily be fallen upon, but we daresay it will be found, in this as in other matters, that the simplest means are best.

Some unkind remarks have recently been made regarding the want of intelligence shown by fishermen in following their calling. They are accused of knowing nothing, or at least very little, about the natural history and habits of the animals they capture ; the accusation is most gratuitous, seeing that it is by means of their knowledge—be it much or little—that we obtain all the fish which are brought to market. The writer in his time has passed many days with the fisher folk, and has found them with regard to their

"Chambers's Journal," Feby. 18, 1882.

occupation just about as intelligent as others of the working class with whom he has been brought into contact, and with far more natural shrewdness, and no men are more ready in a time of peril to do all they know to save a life Now that the means of education have reached even the remotest fishing villages, we shall soon find the rising generations of fishermen upsides with their more learned brethren of those inland towns which have provided literary institutes and free libraries for behoof of the artisans and labourers who inhabit them, and many of whom a few years ago were as ignorant as our fishermen are accused of being to-day.

With improved harbour accommodation and more steam power to aid them in their business, and both of these "wants" we are pleased to know are in course of being gradually supplied, the fisher folk of all grades will find their condition ameliorated and their future looking brighter. We heartily wish them more of the sunshine of life and less of its storms : they have been at all times a gallant, although a peculiar people, and now that attention has been roused to their condition, we trust their earnings will be increased and their sanitary surroundings improved, and that the dangers attending their calling will be fewer in the future than they have been in the past : in that hope we close this imperfect record of "the round of fisher life and labour."

Printed in Great Britain
by Amazon.co.uk, Ltd.,
Marston Gate.